The Common Writer

The Common Writer

Theory and Practice

for

Writers and Teachers

Robert Neale

Auckland
OXFORD UNIVERSITY PRESS
Oxford   New York   Toronto   Melbourne

Oxford University Press, Walton Street, Oxford OX2 6DP
Oxford   New York   Toronto
Delhi   Bombay   Calcutta   Madras   Karachi
Kuala Lumpur   Singapore   Hong Kong   Tokyo
Nairobi   Dar es Salaam   Cape Town
Melbourne   Auckland   Madrid
and associated companies in
Berlin   Ibadan

Oxford is a trade mark of Oxford University Press

First published 1991
Reprinted 1993
© Robert Neale 1991

ISBN 0 19 558221 7

Cover designed by Chris O'Brien
Photoset in Bembo by Rennies Illustrations Ltd.
and printed in Hong Kong
Published by Oxford University Press
1A Matai Road, Greenlane, Auckland 5, New Zealand

For Janet and Alison

CONTENTS

INTRODUCTION

We live in an exploding universe of information. The date of the Big Bang that started it all remains open to debate – perhaps when the ancient Sumerians developed the earliest cuneiform writing in Mesopotamia five and a half thousand years ago, or when paper was invented in China in the second century A.D., or when Johann Gutenberg invented the movable-type printing press in the fifteenth century, or even in the twentieth when the silicon chip put the power of the computer at the disposal of the common writer.

Perhaps the point is academic. What does matter is that writing of one sort or another has been going on for a long time, and shows no sign of passing out of fashion. As the world in the late twentieth century seems to be loosening itself up politically and economically, increasing its emphasis on the freedom, dignity, and (in consequence) responsibility of the individual, so that individual, in order to contribute to society, needs the wherewithal to communicate. For that purpose writing remains by far the most common medium as well as the handiest. Indeed, today's precariously balanced mass-economies render the ability to write essential for survival. Furthermore, like Alice's famous run in Looking-Glass land, where *it takes all the running you can do, to stay in the same place,* getting a job, holding it and making one's mark in the structure of society seem to demand not only advanced writing skills but their continual upgrading. More and more commercial enterprises therefore call in 'consultants' to refurbish their employees' writing abilities, and university and other courses in writing attract increasingly heavy enrolments.

This book responds to that demand in a way rather different from most. It seeks to put into practice several basic principles:

- writing records language, and we will therefore write more effectively if we know something about the way language works

- language creates meaning, so that all writing (whether explicitly 'creative' or not) makes demands on the writer's creativity

- meaning exists, but in the enormously complex interrelationship between speaker/writer, language, text and audience, so that like the rainbow it gleams for ever beyond our reach

- writers learn best to write by writing, and (like everyone else) respond better to example than to precept

- the people most worth listening to about writing are those who do it best – the great writers, in fact.

This book therefore begins by exploring broad issues like mimesis and meaning, irony and subjectivity – all central to the operations of language whether spoken or written, though always affected in special ways by the permanency writing bestows on language. It then briefly examines the writing process, while trying (not always successfully) to resist the temptation to pontificate about how that should be pursued. It then looks briefly at the historical processes that have shaped the writing we do and the language we of the English-speaking world do it in today – again in the faith that understanding helps generate expertise. And it concludes with some suggestions, distilled from my own experience over a good many years as a teacher, about how this expertise may best be passed to the next generation. For all these topics it turns wherever feasible to the experience of distinguished writers, taking their wisdom to be relevant beyond the periods and particular genres they wrote in. The Bibliography lists these sources.

The book stands indebted to a multitude of people: to the many hundreds of my students at Massey University, who have tolerated my stumbling articulation of these ideas, and indeed contributed notably to their refinement over a number of years; to my colleagues, both full and part-time, in the English Department, for countless conversations and generous contributions to my Writing Resource file; to the late Professor R. G. Frean in particular, whose deep and astonishingly fertile mind originated more of this book's material than I care to admit even to myself; to Anne French and the New Zealand staff of Oxford University Press for their apparently inexhaustible enthusiasm, encouragement and expertise; to my daughters, who have unwittingly provided some of the more interesting bits of the book and to whom it is dedicated with all love and due respect; and above all to my wife, who makes it (and everything) worthwhile.

Robert Neale

ACKNOWLEDGEMENTS

I would like to record my gratitude to the following for permission, usually granted with generosity and promptitude, to quote extracts from certain copyright material:

The British Library: Albertine Gaur, *A History of Writing* 1984.

City Lights Books, San Francisco: Ernest Fenollosa, *The Chinese Written Character as a Medium for Poetry,* © Ezra Pound 1936.

J. M. Dent & Sons: *The Mabinogion* trans. Gwyn Jones and Thomas Jones 1949.

Faber & Faber: T. S. Eliot, *Complete Poems and Plays 1909–1950.* Ted Hughes, *The Hawk in the Rain* 1957. Ezra Pound, *ABC of Reading* 1951.

Professor Northrop Frye: *3 Lectures: University of Toronto Installation Lectures,* 1958.

The Hamlyn Publishing Group: Winston Churchill, *My Early Life* 1959.

Henry Holt & Co: Robert Frost, 'Education by Poetry: A Meditative Monologue'.

Hodder & Stoughton and Alfred A. Knopf Inc: Irina Ratushinskaya, *Grey is the Colour of Hope* 1988.

Methuen Children's Books and E. P. Dutton: A. A. Milne, *Winnie the Pooh* 1926.

Mrs Cornelia Myers: L. M. Myers, *The Roots of Modern English* 1966.

The estate of the late Sonia Brownell Orwell and Martin Secker & Warburg Ltd: George Orwell, *Politics and the English Language* 1950 and *Why I Write* 1954.

Oxford University Press: Christopher Fry, *A Phoenix Too Frequent* 1949.

Oxford University Press (NZ): Lauris Edmond, *Selected Poems* 1984.

Penguin Books Ltd: Margaret Lane, *The Tale of Beatrix Potter,* © Frederick Warne & Co., 1946, 1985.

Peters Fraser & Dunlop: Arthur Koestler, *Arrow in the Blue* 1952.

Random Century New Zealand Ltd: Janet Frame, *The Envoy from Mirror City* 1985.

Reinhardt Books: Helen Bannerman, *The Story of Little Black Sambo* 1954.

A. P. Watt Ltd. on behalf of The Trustees of the Robert Graves Copyright Trust: Robert Graves, two versions of the final stanza of 'To Juan at the Winter Solstice' taken from *Collected Poems* 1975.

The estate of P. G. Wodehouse, Messrs. Hutchinson and A. P. Watt Ltd: P. G. Wodehouse, letter to Bill Townend in *Wodehouse on Wodehouse* 1980.

The Executors of the Virginia Woolf Estate and The Hogarth Press: Virginia Woolf, *A Writer's Diary* 1958.

1

MIMESIS

. . . the general principle that Life imitates Art far
more than Art imitates Life.

Oscar Wilde

When we use language, we usually assume we are speaking or writing about
something in the world outside us, or within our own feelings or experience,
or possibly in both. Even a book like this one, which I am writing about
writing, is about not only what my fingers are creating on the screen of my
word processor right now but, I hope, a great many more matters that
regularly concern 'the common writer' everywhere. Language, we feel,
imitates (or describes, or represents, or copies, or refers to) something that
already exists, in its own right, before language comes into being. Whether
this is really the case, and just how language operates – questions, in other
words, of **mimesis** – form the subject of this chapter.

All discussions of mimesis start with the Greek philosopher, Aristotle
(384–322 B.C.), who comments briefly on the subject in the document
known as the *Poetics*. There he suggests that artefacts like pictures and plays
are imitations of something in life, and that we enjoy them – even if they
imitate painful or unpleasant things – because in experiencing them we learn
something about what they imitate: and everybody enjoys learning. Hence
the development of 'creative writing', and our enjoyment of it. Thinkers
since Aristotle, especially from Renaissance times onward, have explored
the subject in various ways. Sir Philip Sidney, defending literature in the
sixteenth century against the puritanical charge that it tells lies, stresses its
mimetic aspect and maintains that no one but a fool would expect it to
'affirm' – that is, to be literally true; all sensible people *know* fiction is fiction.
The eighteenth century English philosopher, John Locke, points out with
painstaking care in his *Essay Concerning Human Understanding* that words bear
no hard and fast relationship to external things at all: if they did, the world
could have only one language, anchored into the things of which it is made

up. If words represent anything, argues Locke, they represent the ideas in our heads, and only those ideas. His formidable contemporary, Jonathan Swift, pursues the same notion in the third Book of *Gulliver's Travels* bringing Gulliver, on a visit to the Grand Academy of Lagado in the land of Balnibarbi, into contact with some 'sages' who had clearly not enjoyed the benefit of reading Locke:

> We next went to the School of Languages, where three Professors sat in Consultation upon improving that of their own Country.
>
> The first Project was to shorten Discourse by cutting Polysyllables into one, and leaving out Verbs and Participles; because in Reality all Things imaginable are but Nouns.
>
> The other, was a Scheme for entirely abolishing all Words whatsoever: And this was urged as a great Advantage in Point of Health as well as Brevity. For, it is plain, that every Word we speak is in some Degree a Diminution of our Lungs by Corrosion; and consequently contributes to the shortning of our Lives. An Expedient was therefore offered, that since Words are only Names for *Things,* it would be more convenient for all Men to carry about with them, such *Things* as were necessary to express the particular Business they are to discourse on. And this Invention would certainly have taken Place, to the great Ease as well as Health of the Subject, if the Women in Conjunction of the Vulgar and Illiterate had not threatened to raise a Rebellion, unless they might be allowed the Liberty to speak with their Tongues, after the Manner of their Forefathers: Such constant irreconcileable Enemies to Science are the common People. However, many of the most Learned and Wise adhere to the new Scheme of expressing themselves by *Things;* which hath only this Inconvenience attending it; that if a Man's Business be very great, and of various Kinds, he must be obliged in Proportion to carry a greater Bundle of *Things* upon his Back, unless he can afford one or two strong Servants to attend him. I have often beheld two of these Sages almost sinking under the Weight of their Packs, like Pedlars among us; who when they met in the Streets would lay down their Loads, open their Sacks, and hold Conversation for an Hour together; then put up their Implements, help each other to resume their Burthens, and take their Leave.
>
> But, for short Conversations, a Man may carry Implements in his Pockets and under his Arms, enough to supply him, and in his House he cannot be at a Loss; therefore the Room where Company meet who practise this Art, is full of all *Things* ready at Hand, requisite to furnish Matter for this Kind of artificial Converse.[1]

Swift's irony not only drives the point home, but makes fools of us if we refuse to agree with him. But one of the reasons why the irony bites so sharply is that we so often catch ourselves behaving as if his sages were right

– not by heaving loads of demonstration material on our backs but by assuming that somehow the word we use postulates a pre-existent thing. "Will you please put that over there?" we ask, trusting that the phrases "that" and "over there" will in some fashion clarify themselves in our hearer's mind (they never do). And we often assume that the existence of words like *gravity, time* and *death* must imply the existence of the equivalent *things* which we could – hypothetically at least – counteract, tame or abolish, to the great satisfaction of writers of science fiction. Some people make similar assumptions about their sacred documents, insisting that the words in the Bible describing Creation, or those in the Koran depicting Paradise, derive their value from whatever historical or factual realities they purport to represent. On a more mundane level which of us, faced with someone who does not understand English, has not been tempted to break through the barrier of incomprehension by reiterating our words more loudly and slowly – as if magnifying the words will somehow render the thing more accessible? And we all know people trapped in the toils of their own jargon who seem quite unaware that alternative, and possibly better, ways of describing the world exist.

This naive view of how language works seems very deep-seated. Perhaps we pick it up in infancy as we begin to learn to talk. It survives powerfully in some cultures in the belief that to know the name of a person or thing is to have control over it: wise people thus keep their 'true names' secret and use some nickname or pseudonym for safety's sake. It retained considerable currency in the Middle Ages as a basis for the philosophical system known as scholasticism. Although the popular image of scholastic philosophers sitting round debating how many angels could dance on the head of a pin does less than justice to many centuries of learned and subtle thought, scholastic philosophy eventually had to be dislodged from its entrenched **realism** (the technical term for this notion that words are inextricably connected to things).

Under the championship of scholars like Peter Abelard the opposite view, known as **nominalism,** insisted upon the essential gap between the words we use and any reality they purport to describe, thus leaving people free to explore both language and nature as separate realities in their own right and to develop new languages, like the formulae of science or the symbols of mathematics, in order to say new things about the world. The rise of nominalism, that is to say, parallels – or perhaps stimulates – the rise of science, and the great age of rational and scientific enquiry, the eighteenth century, is the age of nominalism. We have already seen John Locke and Jonathan Swift endorsing it. The greatest literary figure of the age, Dr

Johnson, encapsulates it with characteristic succinctness: "I am not yet so lost to lexicography as to forget that *words are the daughters of earth, and that things are the sons of heaven.*"[2]

The debate remains unresolved. Indeed in some ways the wheel has come full circle and hypothesis recrystallized into dogma: scratch many a scientist and you will find a 'realist' underneath, attributing to the sign systems of science something of the same absolute validity that scholastic philosophers attached to words. "Scientists are people who really matter" and "Chemists are people of real substance" proclaimed two bumper-stickers on a car I parked next to while shopping at lunchtime today. But if we argue that words are not clearly attached to the things they seem to describe, can we talk about the real world, or our experience of it, with any certainty at all? And if words enjoy a separate and independent existence of their own, then presumably they rate as *things* in their own right, quite as inscrutable as anything else – perhaps more so, since we have to use words to talk about words, making confusion worse confounded. Such problems of discourse have in recent years been subject to vigorous debate of a kind that bridges the traditional subject gap between philosophy and literary criticism; much perplexity and much illumination have been generated.

Most writers today would probably feel they face a choice not between realist and nominalist theories of language, but one within the nominalist position: if we accept John Locke's contention that words stand for our ideas, we then have to ask whether the ideas *can* take shape before we find the words to fit them, or whether words are necessary to the very existence of ideas. Are *words* and *ideas* different things, or the same thing under two different titles? Two conflicting twentieth century views of the problem demonstrate its urgency and complexity. The first comes from George Orwell's influential essay *Politics and the English Language:*

> When you think of a concrete object, you think wordlessly, and then, if you want to describe the thing you have been visualizing you probably hunt about till you find the exact words that seem to fit it. When you think of something abstract you are more inclined to use words from the start, and unless you make a conscious effort to prevent it, the existing dialect will come rushing in and do the job for you, at the expense of blurring or even changing your meaning. Probably it is better to put off using words as long as possible and get one's meaning as clear as one can through pictures or sensations. Afterwards one can choose – not simply *accept* – the phrases that will best cover the meaning, and then switch round and decide what impression one's words are likely to make on another person. This last effort of the mind cuts out all stale or mixed images, all prefabricated phrases, needless repetitions, and humbug and vagueness generally.[3]

The Canadian scholar, critic and ecclesiastic Northrop Frye, on the other hand, seems to take a rather different view:

> In the past, and under the influence of the old faculty psychology, the different fields of study were correlated with different parts of the mind. Thus history was ascribed to the memory, poetry to the imagination, and philosophy and science to the reason. This way of thinking has left many traces in our day: it is still widely believed that a mathematician is an unemotional reasoner, and a poet a "genius", a word which usually means emotionally unbalanced. But, of course, any difficult study demands the whole mind, not pieces of it. Reason and a sense of fact are as important to the novelist as they are to the chemist; genius and creative imagination play the same role in mathematics that they do in poetry. A similar fallacy may be confusing our student at this critical point. I am, he perhaps feels, a conscious being; I know I can think; I know I have ideas that are waiting to be put into words. I wish somebody would show me how to express my ideas, instead of shoving all this poetry at me. After all, poets put their *feelings* into words, so they can make sounds and pictures out of them; but that isn't what I want.
>
> Every step in this chain of reasoning is wrong, so it is no wonder if the reasoner is confused. In the first place, thinking is not a natural process like eating or sleeping. The difficulty here is partly semantic: we are apt to speak of all our mental processes as forms of thought. Musing, day-dreaming, associating, remembering, worrying: every slop and gurgle of our mental sewers we call thinking. If we are asked a question and can only guess at the answer, we begin with the words "I think". But real thinking is an acquired skill founded on practice and habit, like playing the piano, and how well we can think at any given time will depend on how much of it we have already done. Nor can we think at random: we can only add one more idea to the body of something we have already thought about. In fact we, as individuals or egos, can hardly be said to think at all: we link our minds to an objective body of thought, follow its facts and processes, and finally, if the links are strong enough, our minds become a place where something new in the body of thought comes to light.
>
> It is the same with the imaginative thinking of literature. The great writer seldom regards himself as a personality with something to say: his mind to him is simply a place where something happens to words. T.S. Eliot compares the poet to a catalyzer, which accompanies but does not bring about the processes it is used for; Keats speaks of the poet's negative capability; Wordsworth of his recollection in tranquility; Milton of the dictation of unpremeditated verse by a Muse. The place where the greatest fusions of words have occurred in English was in the mind of Shakespeare, and Shakespeare, as a personality, was so self-effacing that he has irritated some people into a frenzy of trying to prove that he never existed.
>
> If the student were studying natural science, he would grasp this principle of objective thought very quickly. There can be no self-expressive approach

to physics or chemistry: one has to learn the laws of the science first before one can have anything to express on it. But the same thing is true of the verbal disciplines. The student is not really struggling with his own ideas, but with the laws and principles of words. In any process of genuine thought that involves words, there can be no such thing as an inarticulate idea waiting to have words put around it. The words are the forms of which the ideas are the content, and until the words have been found, the idea does not exist.[4]

"Think wordlessly" for as long as you can, suggests Orwell. "Until the words have been found, the idea does not exist," counters Frye. In spite of this obvious disagreement, we may partially reconcile the two by noting that Professor Frye finds it necessary to define his terms most carefully, limiting the sense of the word *thought* far more rigorously than common usage suggests. But George Orwell is also talking about some kind of systematic attempt to "get one's meaning clear," and is not merely appropriating the "slop and gurgle of our mental sewers" that Frye explicitly excludes from his definition. It would be comfortable to conclude that both views represent a partial truth, or different sides of a paradoxical reality; but each view has practical repercussions for us as writers, and we cannot follow the advice of both at once. They may of course be thinking of different types of writing, though neither makes it quite clear what he has in mind. Perhaps Orwell's advice may be more useful for someone writing a knitting pattern or an engineering manual, Frye's for someone undertaking an academic research paper. In the end, we must submit their claims to the trial of our own experience and assess them in the context of the kind of writing we do.

Both men, oddly enough, put forward their theories as part of a campaign for urging writers towards greater responsibility and independence. This common purpose perhaps, in the end, outweighs any of the differences between them, and points to our next consideration in this discussion of mimesis: whenever we write anything (other than a verbatim copy) we not only imitate something that perhaps already exists but also make something new. Aristotle calls this **poesis**, a noun derived from the Greek verb meaning *to make*, which also gives us the word *poet*. The notion of *poet* as *maker* is a very old one: the two words were interchangeable in most medieval English dialects, and we acknowledge the idea in our term *creative writing*.

The current debate about discourse I mentioned earlier leans very markedly towards this view of language. Most of its participants would probably endorse and extend the theory of mimesis put forward by Northrop Frye, arguing that words *make* the world: they shape our ideas about the world, and our ideas are all we have to go on. The example most commonly advanced for this view is that of the rainbow, which consists (presumably) of a band of colour changing at a constant and uniform rate from one side of the visible spectrum to the other. Yet people who think in English see in it the seven stripes – of red, orange, yellow, green, blue, indigo and violet – which our vocabulary identifies (though I have always had problems with indigo, perhaps because of some ocular deficiency). Scholars have identified other languages that name more or fewer colours with the presumed result that their speakers actually see the rainbow differently. Dr Johnson would today have to say "if words are the daughters of the mind, then things are the sons of words" and we may well recall the proclamation that opens St John's Gospel: "In the beginning was the Word". To put it another way, we have moved from Aristotle's view that Art imitates Life to Oscar Wilde's contention, explored in his critical essay *The Decay of Lying*, that Life imitates Art.[5]

If words thus shape the world we live in, then what we do with them matters very much indeed: if you get the words right, the things will look after themselves. Hence, presumably, the constant efforts of politicians to find *formulae* – forms of words to which all parties to a dispute can assent. Hence too the frequent claims of poets to immortalize someone – usually a beloved – in verse. Language can create, and therefore language can sustain:

> Not marble, nor the guilded monuments
> Of Princes shall out-live this powrefull rime,
> But you shall shine more bright in these contents
> Than unswept stone, besmeer'd with sluttish time.
> When wastefull warre shall *Statues* over-turne,
> And broiles roote out the worke of masonry,
> Nor *Mars* his sword, nor warres quick fire shall burne:
> The living record of your memory.
> Gainst death, and all oblivious enmity
> Shall you pace forth, your praise shall stil finde roome,
> Even in the eyes of all posterity
> That weare this world out to the ending doome.
>   So til the judgement that your selfe arise,
>   You live in this, and dwell in lovers eies.[6]

Today's scholarly debate therefore understandably concentrates on the words themselves rather than on any *things* to which they might be taken to refer. In its earlier stages it explored the shape of the word-structures a writer builds, and looked for meaning and impact in the patterns, echoes, resonances and so on that emerge; more recently people have remarked on the problems of ambiguity and uncertainty that arise when any individual writer undertakes a construction job with words none of which, by necessity, belongs to that writer alone – they are the common property of us all, indeed spanning more generations than ours, and every single one of them has wider implications than we can ever grasp: how much further beyond our reach, therefore, is anything made of a multiplicity of them.

Nevertheless, for all these intractable problems, we still want, or need, to write; and we have to use language while doing so. Some awareness of the mimetic and poetic functions of language will help us adopt the responsible and thoughtful approach to writing that both George Orwell and Northrop Frye urge us to take. Even then, language probably gets its own way in the long run: we can write down only those ideas for which words exist, and assemble those ideas only in the relationships which our grammar permits. The diction of other languages allows other meanings: English *boy* is not quite the same as French *garçon*, and Maori *mana* subtly but perceptibly different from English *prestige*. Latin grammar allows you to say things you cannot say in English, and vice versa. We will explore these limitations further in Chapter 9 when we trace the way English grammar and vocabulary have changed over the centuries.

English syntax limits us in the same way by artificially dividing the whole of perceived reality into three categories: stationary and eternal *things*, which the language represents by means of nouns; certain static and detachable *attributes* of these things, conveyed by adjectives; and a *state of flux* in which all these things and their attributes may be involved, expressed by verbs. Other parts of speech like adverbs, prepositions, conjunctions and so on merely serve to undergird these extraordinary and highly suspect divisions. Furthermore our syntax forces us to express all our ideas within its inescapable subject-verb-object (or subject-predicate) structure. We may just be able to conceive of an alternative structure existing, but, unless acquainted with some language (outside the Indo-European family) that does things differently, we find it hard to imagine how that alternative could operate: our grammar makes us see the world as things operating on other things – a state of affairs, if you think about it, with rather sobering overtones. Novelist Janet Frame, in *The Envoy from Mirror City* (the third volume of her autobiography) writes of "one of the great themes of fiction – the gift, the giver, the receiver and the thing received, a theme so basic it is embedded in the grammar and syntax of the language where it lies like a trap or a shaft of light.[7]"

As that final "shaft of light" suggests, we need not feel entirely enslaved by the language. Even within the boundaries of conventional syntax there lie many different worlds that the writer can present or represent. A few examples may suggest some possibilities:

> And on the morrow Peredur arose and equipped himself and his horse to go to the tournament. And he could see a pavilion amongst the other pavilions, the fairest he had ever seen. And he could see a fair maiden craning her head through a window of the pavilion. And he had never seen a fairer maiden, and a robe of gold brocaded silk about her. And he looked hard at the maiden, and great love of her entered into him.
>
> anon., *Peredur Son of Efrawg* (ca. 11c., transl. Gwyn and Thomas Jones)[8]

> Once upon a time there was a little black boy, and his name was little Black Sambo. And his Mother was called Black Mumbo. And his Father was called Black Jumbo. And Black Mumbo made him a beautiful little Red Coat, and a pair of beautiful little Blue Trousers. And Black Jumbo went to the Bazaar, and bought him a beautiful Green Umbrella, and a lovely little Pair of Purple Shoes with Crimson Soles and Crimson Linings. And then wasn't Little Black Sambo grand?
>
> Helen Bannerman, *The Story of Little Black Sambo* (1899)[9]

> This morning there *were* letters – letters which had reached London, apparently all together, the day of Strether's journey, and had taken their time to follow him; so that, after a controlled impulse to go into them in the reception-room of the bank, which, reminding him of the post office at Woollett, affected him as the abutment of some transatlantic bridge, he slipped them into the pocket of his loose grey overcoat with a sense of the felicity of carrying them off.
>
> Henry James, *The Ambassadors* (1904)[10]

Apart from the fact that they all tell a story, these three seem to have little in common. They represent widely separate genres (Celtic romance, Victorian children's book and American psychological novel) and share only a very general structure in which linked details move towards a climax – Peredur's falling in love, Little Black Sambo's sartorial splendour and Strether's happy departure with his letters. In the manner of linking its details *Little Black Sambo* stands much nearer to the medieval Welsh tale than to the novel, even though Henry James and Helen Bannerman were contemporaries. This manner is **paratactic**: all the component parts, that is to say, make contributions of about the same weight and arrive in steady sequence, linked for the most part by co-ordinating conjunctions (usually *and*). **Parataxis** provides little or no depth of analysis; we skate smoothly along the surface of the narrative – indeed we move in a world of surfaces, where concealed motives, or cause and effect of any kind, remain unheard of or have to grow by implication outside the actual words. To find out if anything else is going on in the first passage we have to respond to hints like the repetition of *pavilion* and of the word *fair* in its various forms, and the parallel between "the robe of gold brocaded silk" about the maiden and the "great love of her" that enters Peredur – the style characteristically draws no distinction between inner and outer qualities. *Little Black Sambo* too contains elaborate repetition and parallelism, but apart from contributing something to Little Black Sambo's naive grandeur these exist, as far as I can see, purely for their own sake – for the fun children find in this kind of thing – rather than to generate any further meaning.

The paratactic style adumbrates a world – a world characteristic perhaps of the medieval Romance or the children's story – where all is as it seems to be and few profound questions of human motivation or duplicity disturb us. But it is also the world of classical epic, of some kinds of tragedy and of the macabre, where event succeeds event in mindless and unstoppable sequence and there is little that impotent humanity can do about it except perhaps go down with colours flying.

Its opposite, the **hypotactic** style, represents a world of a different sort – one of order and subordination, whose component parts hold and map each other like the pieces of a jigsaw puzzle. To achieve this it relies heavily on grammatical subordination, exploiting the astonishing variety of English clause and phrase types and the wide range of punctuation available to the modern writer. Henry James controls the passage quoted from *The Ambassadors* partly by skilful use of dash, comma, semi-colon and italics, and partly by means of subordinating conjunctions like *which* and *so that*. As a result he can do very complicated things with his time-scheme, moving effortlessly from present to recent past to present to remoter past, finally returning to the immediate present as Strether moves off with the letters in his pocket. And this temporal journeying has mostly been traced through Strether's consciousness: we have learnt a little bit more about him in things like the emphasis on the italicized *were*, the phrase "had taken their time" and so on. While his "loose grey overcoat" works in some ways to define him (as Peredur's maiden's "robe of gold brocaded silk" defines her) the references to "the post office at Woollett" and "the abutment of some translantic bridge" presumably possess some ironic significance contingent, no doubt, upon our acquaintance with the earlier part of the novel. In the world of **hypotaxis**, everything fits, and it becomes the writer's reponsibility to articulate the patterns and relationships that hold the world together.

Most writing, of course, contains both paratactic and hypotactic elements; co-ordination and subordination can happily co-exist, as they are doing in this paragraph so far. Nor are these styles applicable only to narrative writing: my weekly shopping list properly demonstrates an extreme parataxis of a sort that I would deplore in a student essay or indeed in any piece of literary criticism, which is by nature a hypotactic art. The writer needs to choose whichever style imitates, or creates, the most appropriate reality.

The kinds of verb we choose also matter a good deal. We saw earlier in this chapter that in English, as indeed in all Indo-European languages, the verbs represent that side of reality we believe to be on the move – the flux of the world, as it were, rather than the stasis (whch is what the nouns look after). The concept of pure noun, *things doing nothing*, is an improbable one; nothing simply *is*. Reality, so far as we can conceive of it, consists of *things in action* – and the *things* are ultimately inseparable from the *actions*.

> A true noun, an isolated thing, does not exist in nature. Things are only the terminal points, or rather the meeting points of actions, cross-sections cut through actions, snap-shots. Neither can a pure verb, an abstract motion, be possible in nature. The eye sees noun and verb as one: things in motion, motion in things . . .[11]

Every noun, that is to say, and every verb, represents an unacceptable oversimplification of the truth. But these, together with a few subordinate parts of speech, are all we have, and we must make the best of it.

One way of doing so is to opt, unless we have very good reasons not to, for **active verbs** – as I have done in this sentence (I could have written "This can *be done* if choice *is made* of active verbs, unless good reason *is discovered* to the contrary" – the passive verbs are italicized). Active verbs compensate for the deficiencies of English syntax better than passive ones do; at least they represent *things doing things* rather than *things having things done to them*. As writers we often choose passive verb forms out of laziness or ignorance: they demand less effort because they convey less information, saying what was done but not who did it. But for the same reason they demand more effort from the reader, and we choose them at our peril. They may come in handy to the ironist, who often wants readers to draw their own (perhaps uncomfortable) conclusions; Swift uses them thus in the excerpt from *Gulliver's Travels* we examined earlier. Or writers may turn to them in order to convey an emphasis they cannot otherwise achieve. But passive verbs accomplish little else, and form one of the most deplorable features of the writing of scientists, whose heavy reliance on them perhaps stems from a vague (and mistaken) feeling that saying "the results were tabulated" proclaims the writer's objectivity and modesty better than saying "I (or my assistant, or research team) tabulated the results". We will discuss objectivity and subjectivity in Chapter 6.

Passive verb forms also rob our writing of a good deal of interesting colour, consisting as they do of some form of the verb *to be* with an adjective in tow. The verb *to be*, because of its universal applicability, lacks specific bite: everything *is*. But most things do a lot of things besides merely *being*, and we can usually make our writing more interesting to our readers, and perhaps find out more about what we really want to say, by spending time and effort looking for appropriate active verbs.

> This [the *universal copula "is"*] is an ultimate weakness of language. It has come from generalizing all intransitive words into one. As "live," "see," "walk," "breathe," are generalized into states by dropping their objects, so these weak verbs are in turn reduced to the abstractest state of all, namely, bare existence.
>
> There is in reality no such verb as the pure copula, no such original conception, our very word *exist* means "to stand forth" to show oneself by a definite act. "Is" comes from the Aryan root *as*, to breathe. "Be" is from *bhu* to grow . . . I have seldom seen our rhetoricians dwell on the fact that the great strength of our language lies in its splendid array of transitive verbs, drawn both from Anglo-Saxon and from Latin sources. These give us the most individual characterizations of force. Their power lies in their recognition of nature as a vast storehouse of forces. We do not say in English that things seem, or appear, or eventuate, or even that they are; but that they *do*. Will is the foundation of our speech. We catch the Demiurge in the act. I had to discover for myself why Shakespeare's English was so immeasurably superior to all others. I found that it was his persistent, natural and magnificent use of hundreds of transitive verbs. Rarely will you find an "is" in his sentences. "Is" weakly lends itself to the uses of our rhythm, in the unaccented syllables; yet he sternly discards it. A study of Shakespeare's verbs should underlie all exercises in style.[12]

As this comment implies, it probably takes some courage as well as imagination to come up with the best verb. When Hamlet asks the Gravedigger "How long will a man lie i' the earth ere he rot?" Shakespeare's choice of final verb shows him unflinchingly acknowledging something that most of us – if we think about it at all – try to wrap up in terms like 'biodegradability' or 'pushing up the daisies'. Perhaps Lauris Edmond tells the truth:

> We recognise the great
> poets by their unshakeable courage[13]

Otherwise cowardice and laziness rule in language as in life, witness the recent communication from my local council informing me that certain trees in our street 'are to be removed and will be replaced by something more suitable'. Who will remove them, and replace them, and when? (And indeed more suitable to whom, or what?)

All the extracts quoted in this chapter set us a good example; the one from *Peredur* uses the active vigour of its verbs to make a positive virtue out of a potentially monotonous sentence structure. Apart from unavoidable references to the verb *to be* I have taken particular care in this paragraph to seek out verbs with more life to them – as indeed I have throughout this book, though no doubt you will find many occasions on which I have nodded. But if we value our moral probity, care for our audience, and want our writing to imitate (or make) a world with some colour and movement in it, such a search pays off. Consider the worlds opened up by the prose of Swift, Orwell, Frye, Henry James, the writer of the *Peredur* extract, and even of Helen Bannerman; then contrast them with the world we encounter in the kind of writing, still too common today, which largely consists of a parade of fluffy, imprecise abstract nouns tacked together by means of *the universal copula 'is'*. Such writing goes by the appropriately hideous name of **nominalization**:

> . . . behaviours will be acquired if they are followed by positive reinforcement or if they are perceived as potentially leading to positive reinforcement. If there are uniformities of personality development, or if it seems that development proceeds in the same way for sizeable groups of persons, it is because there are uniformities in environments, mostly social and cultural, which make available a uniform schedule of reinforcements for a narrow range of behaviours.

Which world would you rather inhabit?

Notes

1 Swift Book III Ch. 5
2 Johnson p.310
3 Orwell *Shooting an Elephant* p.100
4 Frye pp.15-16
5 see Chapter 5
6 Shakespeare *Sonnet* 55
7 Frame p.175
8 *Mabinogion* p.215
9 Bannerman pp.7-19

10 James p.46
11 Fenollosa p.10
12 Fenollosa pp.15,20
13 Edmond p.45

2

METAPHOR

> . . . that interminable building reared
> By observation of affinities
> In objects where no brotherhood exists
> To passive minds
>
> *Wordsworth*

As in the previous chapter, we begin with Aristotle – and again with his *Poetics*. After a discussion of the various kinds of diction available to a writer, he concludes:

> It is a great thing, indeed, to make a proper use of these poetical forms, as also of compounds and strange words. But the greatest thing by far is to be a master of metaphor. It is the one thing that cannot be learnt from others; and it is also a sign of genius, since a good metaphor implies an intuitive perception of the similarity in dissimilars.[1]

Why, we may well wonder, does Aristotle lay such emphasis upon what many of us will have learnt about at school as just another 'figure of speech', along with simile, personification, hyperbole and – if the teacher was up to it – metonymy, synecdoche, oxymoron, zeugma and similar Greek mystifications? To suggest some answers to this question I shall begin this chapter by attempting to define and describe metaphor as fully as possible, and then explore its importance in our language and experience. Its effects on us as writers will become clearer as we go.

One of the most useful definitions of metaphor occurs in a piece of critical biography written in the eighteenth century by its leading man of letters, Dr Samuel Johnson. In his *Life of Cowley* he undertakes an analysis of the 'metaphysical conceit', a particularly marked and sustained kind of metaphor affected by the 'metaphysical' poets, of whom Abraham Cowley was one and John Donne possibly the greatest. Extravagant notions like Donne's famous comparison between two parting lovers and the straddling legs of a pair of compasses well represent the kind of *wit* Johnson is describing, but his remarks identify the essence of metaphor in general:

> . . . wit, abstracted from its effects upon the hearer, may be more rigorously and philosophically considered as a kind of *discordia concors:*[2] a combination of dissimilar images, or discovery of occult resemblances in things apparently unlike. Of wit, thus defined, they [the metaphysical poets] have more than enough. The most heterogenous ideas are yoked by violence together . . .[3]

Metaphor, both Aristotle and Johnson suggest, posits the similarity – indeed the identity or oneness – of two apparently unlike things. In doing this it appeals to something embedded very deep in the human mind. "What is it *like?*" we ask when trying to find out about any new object or experience (unless we are gutter television interviewers, in which case we ask "How does it feel . . .?" – obliquely but palpably denying our interlocutor's rationality and perhaps even humanity). We learn, it seems, by moving to new experiences through the channels of the old, by explaining and interpreting the unfamiliar to ourselves in terms of the familiar. Thus to New Zealand's (comparatively) recently arrived English-speaking population the country's flora and fauna abound with things like beech trees and robins whose similarity to their old-world prototypes, when it came to naming them, outweighed their obvious differences.

Thus language, which must remain relatively static to render communication at all possible, adapts old terms to new things and ideas. The world of computers – especially word-processors with their *menus, windows, files, desk-tops, fonts, clipboards, scrapbooks, rulers, widows, orphans* and so on – provides a particularly rich feast of examples. And the process happens in a wide variety of ways: when Keats writes of "silver snarling trumpets", or of

> Joy, whose hand is ever at his lips,
> Bidding adieu

or when T. S. Eliot notices "the pleasant whining of a mandoline", or Robert Burns claims his love to be "like a red, red rose", we see figures of speech like personification and simile declaring the identity of two dissimilar things and doing a job so like that of metaphor that we may as well regard them as sub-species of the same thing.

According to American poet Robert Frost:

> Poetry begins in trivial metaphors, petty metaphors, "grace" metaphors, and goes on to the profoundest thinking we have. Poetry provides the one

permissible way of saying one thing and meaning another. People say, "Why don't you say what you mean?" We never do that, do we, being all of us too much poets. We like to talk in parables and hints and indirections – whether from diffidence or some other instinct.[4]

All this may well confirm Aristotle's suggestion that metaphor, thus defined, works hardest when language takes its most powerful, condensed and accurate form – poetry. As *Antony and Cleopatra* draws near its climax, Shakespeare demonstrates his power as a poet and some of the qualities of metaphor itself in the astonishing language with which he surrounds the action. Cleopatra's waiting-woman Iras urges her to:

> Finish good lady; the bright day is done
> And we are for the dark.

Cleopatra then kisses Iras, whose subsequent collapse and death prompts the Queen to ask:

> Have I the aspic in my lips? Dost fall?
> If thou and nature can so gently part,
> The stroke of death is as a lover's pinch,
> Which hurts, and is desired.

Cleopatra, who (as Octavius Caesar knows) has "pursued conclusions infinite Of easy ways to die", then applies a poisonous snake to her breast with the words:

> Come, thou mortal wretch
> With thy sharp teeth this knot intrinsicate
> Of life at once untie

and, as the venom works, soothes the anguished Charmian:

> Peace, peace!
> Dost thou not see the baby at my breast,
> That sucks the nurse asleep?

Shakespeare's subject here is nothing less than life itself and its profoundest mystery, death; and he turns with masterly tact to the most mundane comparisons in order to express and explore these inexpressible things. Commonplace experiences like the sequence of day and night, lovers' pinches (in which Cleopatra is an admitted expert), undoing knots with your teeth, and a mother suckling her child – these are the stuff of which Shakespeare makes some of the greatest poetry ever written. Not only does his imagination encompass widely differing experiences and assert their oneness, but he affirms this wholeness by using simple words – *pinch, knot* and so on – in the same breath as the brilliantly contrasting *intrinsicate.* And if you remember Chapter 1 of this book you will already have noticed his direct and sinewy active verbs, each contributing vigour and colour to the metaphors.

The real power of great poetic metaphor like this lies in the way it combines the shock of surprise, the jolt of some new and unexplored comparison, with a sense of absolute rightness. We feel ourselves face to face with truth of the profoundest kind. Aristotle rightly affirms metaphor to be the mark of genius since it shows humanity at its most creative, taking the building blocks of the world and rearranging them into new structures, altering reality as we know it. This is why the Romantic poet Percy Bysshe Shelley called poets "the unacknowledged legislators of the world", and why great writers, whether of poetry or prose, exercise an influence on our society out of all proportion to their numbers.

In a well known passage from *A Midsummer Night's Dream* Shakespeare himself describes the whole process not only memorably but also with the extreme accuracy that only great poetry can achieve:

> The poet's eye, in a fine frenzy rolling,
> Doth glance from heaven to earth, from earth to heaven;
> And, as imagination bodies forth
> The forms of things unknown, the poet's pen
> Turns them to shapes, and gives to airy nothing
> A local habitation and a name.[5]

Few of us, of course, produce more than a handful of such metaphoric insights during the course of our lives. But our thoughts wear the garb of metaphor all the time, as terms like *produce, handful, insights, course* (twice), and *wear the garb* in these two sentences show. A writer can, with care, use language of relatively low metaphoric content, usually in order to achieve a sparse, plain, perfunctory effect of the sort that Jonathan Swift, for example, relies on to deceive us into 'believing' the events described in *Gulliver's Travels.* A glance at the passage quoted in Chapter 1 may find evidence to support Dr Johnson's charge that "the rogue never hazards a metaphor". But even Swift cannot avoid the metaphors lurking in ordinary words: he writes of "*cutting* polysyllables into one", of "*raising* a rebellion", of "*adhering* to a scheme", of "things *furnishing* matter" and so on. If we use words at all, and especially if we pick vigorous verbs and participles of this sort, we have to take constant account of metaphor. Hence Aristotle's emphasis upon the subject and, of course, its inclusion for discussion in this book on writing.

Any metaphor, as our definitions have shown, consists of two parts – though as we shall see later the two do not necessarily make equal contributions. In most metaphors it is relatively easy to distinguish the pre-existing topic, that which we are already talking about, from the new, foreign material we bring in for purposes of contrast and clarification. Scholars call the first of these the **tenor** (it helps to think of it as 'singing the main tune') and the second the **vehicle** (that which conveys a new idea to us). Thus when Swift writes of "cutting polysyllables into one" his tenor is the process of shortening long words into a single syllable, and his vehicle the kind of thing you do with a knife.

This distinction, once made, may seem obvious enough, but clarifying and distinguishing the constituent parts of any metaphor usually demand more practice and experience than we might expect. Children, susceptible to the naive views of mimesis that we saw in the previous chapter, notably lack this experience, and we can all recall the bafflement that results: phrases like 'to put yourself in someone else's shoes', 'to put money on a horse', 'to hold your tongue' and so on have all generated their share of incomprehension within my own experience and family circle. In the wider world disagreement about the exact metaphoric content of Biblical statements like "this is my body" and "the keys of the kingdom of heaven" has led, over the centuries, to bitter and sometimes lethal conflict.

A naively literal response to language not only generates perplexity of this sort but denies some of the central qualities of language. It can frequently result in the entertaining idiocy of mixed metaphor. The perhaps mythical British/Irish parliamentarian Sir Boyle Roche, who declared:

Mr Speaker, I smell a rat. I see it floating in the air, and unless it is nipped in the bud it will unleash a conflagration that will inundate the world

and the almost equally hypothetical schoolmaster who said "if that boy doesn't pull his socks together I shall put the wind of God up him" (and who later described the same boy as "taking his punishment without turning an eyelid") were proclaiming their common ignorance of tenor and vehicle and their common susceptibility to what George Orwell calls the prefabricated phrase.

Mixed metaphor lurks everywhere, sometimes ensnaring those who should know better; in the following paragraph (from a paper on the teaching of English) levers, guns and oysters all indulge in bizarre behaviour:

> The child has vocabulary; he has experiences; he has grammar; and he has his culture. Surely these are worth valuing and preserving. Surely these are worth using as a lever to broader, deeper and richer goals. But more important, perhaps, than the school using what the child brings may be the effect upon the child's self-image of the school's use of what he brings. Dignity and self-respect accompany acceptance of him as he is. Proud of his heritage, he can begin to raise his sights so that his goal will always be just beyond his grasp. On the other hand, if everything he knows is wrong and everything he does is bad, he is apt to close his shell like an oyster and silently drift away to stand against the world of the school rather than with and of it.

But not all mixed metaphor is ludicrous. Shakespeare, making Macbeth describe

> Pity, like a naked new-born babe,
> Striding the blast

or Dylan Thomas writing in *Fernhill* of

> . . . the spellbound horses walking warm
> Out of the whinnying green stable
> On to the fields of praise

both deliberately mix their metaphors to powerful effect. *Naked new-born babes* rarely *stride,* but the vivid picture of one doing so piles metaphor upon metaphor to convey the combination of vulnerability and strength that Shakespeare attributes to Pity. And Dylan Thomas, investing the stable with the sound of the horse and the colour of its fields, reinvests all the terms with a fresh and arresting significance.

Not only do we need to remain alert for the metaphorical potential of ordinary words, but we must accept that this varies enormously from one word to another. Nobody knows, of course, how words began; it is certain, however, that a lot of those we use today contain some measure of pictorial content. We have paused once or twice in this chapter already to consider this – and that word *consider* itself provides an interesting example: the first syllable comes from the Latin word for *with* or *alongside,* while the Oxford Dictionary suggests that the remainder may have descended from Latin *sidereus,* 'starry'. How such a term, perhaps derived from early Roman augury or divination, has made its way into our daily vocabulary makes for fascinating speculation. We could pause over *derive,* too; it originally bore the sense of 'floating away from a river bank'. As for *originally* . . . This study knows no end:

> The whole delicate substance of speech is built upon substrata of metaphor. Abstract terms, pressed by etymology, reveal their ancient roots still embedded in direct action. But the primitive metaphors do not spring from arbitrary subjective processes. They are possible only because they follow objective lines of relations in nature herself. Relations are more real and more important than the things which they relate . . . Had the world not been full of homologies, sympathies, and identities, thought would have been starved and language chained to the obvious. There would have been no bridge whereby to cross from the minor truth of the seen to the major truth of the unseen. Not more than a few hundred roots out of our large vocabularies could have dealt directly with physical processes. These we can fairly well identify in primitive Sanskrit. They are, almost without exception, vivid verbs. The wealth of European speech grew, following slowly the intricate maze of nature's suggestions and affinities. Metaphor was piled upon metaphor in quasi-geological structure.[6]

Pressed by etymology, even parts of words may hold some tiny pictorial residue: the common adverbial suffix *-ly,* for example, descends lineally, by way of the word *like,* from the Anglo-Saxon word for *body,* which itself survives in modern English only in the term *lych-gate* (the name for the covered gateway outside some churches and funeral parlours under which pall bearers were expected to rest the coffin). If we act courageous*ly,* therefore, we are acting courageous-*like* – with, as it were, a *body* of courage; the adverbial form arose from some such essentially metaphorical view.

We see in all this not only the process of semantic shift (which we will discuss more fully in Chapter 9) but a gradual draining of pictorial content from words. Whatever the Romans thought about it, we no longer see river banks when we use the word *derive.* To sustain this kind of verbal image takes more effort than we usually seem inclined to devote to language, and much of our vocabulary seems to be steadily reverting to a species of grey sludge – though perhaps new metaphoric coinages of the sort made by the computer industry partly compensate for this.

Our ancestors built the accumulations of metaphor into structures of

language and into systems of thought. Languages today are thin and cold because we think less and less into them. We are forced, for the sake of quickness and sharpness, to file down each word to its narrowest edge of meaning. Nature would seem to have become less like a paradise and more and more like a factory. We are content to accept the vulgar misuse of the moment.
A late stage of decay is arrested and embalmed in the dictionary.
Only scholars and poets feel painfully back along the thread of our etymologies and piece together our diction, as best they may, from forgotten fragments.[7]

T. S. Eliot, for example, can exploit a deft ironic pun to reinvigorate a word grown tired (mostly in the service of education) when he makes J. Alfred Prufrock seek

> . . . time yet for a hundred indecisions
> And for a hundred visions and **revisions**
> Before the taking of a toast and tea

This kind of thing shows a heightened awareness of the distinction between *tenor* and *vehicle,* in strong contrast with the obtuseness of people like Sir Boyle Roche. He, poor man, has very little idea at all about what he is saying, and must remain an object-lesson to us all about the lure and danger of the **cliché**, a common outcome of our habitual mental lassitude. The term describes metaphor moribund beyond the help even of the kind of cardio-pulmonary resuscitation we have just seen Eliot applying – metaphor in which the illuminating spark no longer leaps between vehicle and tenor; indeed in cliché the distinction between the two has totally collapsed.

The use of cliché sets in motion a vicious downward spiral of disintegrating meaning: we use them because we cannot be bothered to work out our meaning for ourselves, and as we use them they increasingly prevent us, as they prevented Sir Boyle Roche, from meaning anything at all. In a society afflicted with under-educated journalists we become habituated to hearing television and radio news-items claiming that "some snags remain to be ironed out", or that "grass-roots are making their voices heard". For writers like this, nothing ever 'stops' – it 'grinds to a halt'; and people never 'say nothing' – they always 'remain tight lipped' (a demanding and uncomfortable attitude if you sustain it for more than a few seconds). Few of us remain innocent of such vapidities: we may all nowadays feel a little self-conscious about inserting 'the thin end of the wedge' or failing 'to see the wood for the trees', but 'the tip of the iceberg' retains its universal appeal and we seem to be hearing more and more about 'the bottom line'.

And we must all share the blame for the downward slide of the once vigorous and colourful verb *involve,* which meant something like *entangle* (you could get *involved,* physically or metaphorically – or, no doubt, both at once – with a member of the opposite sex). Now we all use the word, out of laziness, to indicate some loosely conceived connexion between whatever two things we are talking about: 'this job involves some overtime'; 'she is involved in hospital administration' and so on. The word *situation* often occurs in the neighbourhood of *involve,* and we overuse it in the same way: educationalists talk pompously of 'the classroom situation' when they mean the classroom, and we hear similarly of 'office situations', 'ward situations' 'emergency situations' and the like. There are few writing situations involving the words *involve* and *situation* where both cannot be thrown out to the benefit of both writer and reader. And plenty of other clichés lie in wait to muddle our thinking and tease our readers. Responsible writers should make their own list of the bad habits that regularly allure them.

Language thus offers us vast resources of metaphor which we ignore at our peril. We may even face the possibility that language itself works as one gigantic metaphor. One of the views of mimesis we discussed in Chapter 1 –the view that a separate reality exists of which language can provide only a dim and inadequate imitation – would support this notion. I can produce an apple – the 'real' thing, pips, juice, cellulose, skin, stalk and all – and various kinds of imitation thereof: I can take a photograph, for example; or I can use my vocal cords to set in motion molecular vibrations of the air to push the sound *apple* on to someone else's eardrum and into their consciousness (I don't know at what stage in all this the sound *apple* can be said to exist); or I can write *apple* in one of the many scripts and versions available (APPLE, **apple**, *pomme* etc.), producing a second imitation, this time not directly of the 'real' thing but of the spoken word, and get this copy of a copy into my readers' minds through their optic systems. In all these cases the reality works as the tenor of our metaphor, and the photograph and both kinds of language as vehicles of different sorts – each behaving as the new and fundamentally different thing that we adduce in order to explain or account for the tenor. Whatever its philosophical respectability, this view has its uses in reminding us that whenever we use language we commit ourselves somehow or other to telling lies, at least in the sense that the copy, no matter how hard we work at it, remains fundamentally alien to the original.

Metaphor, indeed, always works like this. We turn to it to discover the truth about some new experience, and it replies with a distortion. If Burns is right, "My love is like a red, red rose" – but in fact she isn't at all; the closest investigation fails to find any trace of the petals, pistils, stamens, stalk, thorns and so on by which we habitually identify a rose. And yet. . . and yet . . . she *is* like a rose, and a *red, red* one at that. At least, to say so tells a more accurate truth about what she means to me than any personality profile or any analysis of her chemical composition, vital statistics or specific gravity could ever manage to convey.

To tell the truth I have had, therefore, to invent a lie – or at least assent to one made up for me by a great poet. Metaphor distorts as well as clarifies; perhaps it clarifies by distorting. We are back with some of the problems of mimesis we faced in the first chapter, and in the light of our findings about metaphor may well prefer to see language as *poesis,* as a making, rather than as an imitation (though I can't help feeling that *my love* was already somehow there even before Burns came along with his *red, red rose*).

Whichever view we favour, there seems no doubt that when we speak of knowing anything we usually mean the kind of indirect knowledge granted by metaphor: we know most things *in terms of other things* rather than directly, as themselves. Perhaps we may make an exception of unmediated physical sensations – at least of pain: if I sit on a drawing-pin I experience it (to start with) wordlessly. But most other experiences, even bodily ones, depend largely on words to shape their meaning for us; and if we want to analyse or discuss them we have nothing but words in which to do so, and must therefore rely in some way or other upon metaphor. We earlier identified figures of speech like personification and simile as refinements of metaphor; the others I also listed, more or less at random, earlier in this chapter, work similarly: metonymy, which identifies the thing by one of its attributes (*blue-collar* workers); synecdoche, which identifies it by one of its parts (*head* of cattle); oxymoron, which identifies it by its opposite (the *darkness visible* of Milton's Hell); and zeugma, which identifies it by pulling it in two directions (*they pursued it with forks and hope*) also constitute ways of expressing something in terms of something different. They, and many other linguistic devices of the same sort behave, that is to say, as subspecies of metaphor, and thus contribute in their various ways to that constant metaphorical exploration of experience that we call (metaphorically, from the tongues in our heads) language.

Metaphor rules. Whether or not you think this OK depends, finally, on your theology. A grasp of the operations of metaphor suggests that no bit of language can do more than hint at the truth. If we think otherwise we make the same mistake as the child pinching its tongue between finger and thumb when told to hold it – the mistake of investing any utterance with an absolute authority combined with an absolute unambiguity. The great words and phrases by which we shape our existence and that of the society we live in have all come into being by process of metaphor; and the bigger the term, the harder we find it to spot both the tenor and the vehicle of that metaphor. In the small metaphors of life, like *shooting some rapids* or *shouting a round of drinks* we do no great damage if we concentrate on the tenor but pay little attention to the vehicle: we survive the white water or get our beer regardless. On the other hand, in the two great social metaphors we have inherited from the nineteenth century, *evolution* and *revolution*, to ignore the idea of *turning* that supplies the vehicle for both exposes us to the danger of forgetting entirely that they are metaphors and treating them as unambiguous statements of reality, which they are not. If we remember their metaphorical essence, we can debate and discuss them like human beings – *think about* them, in fact. If we forget, and invest them with some absolute and unambiguous value, then we can only accept or reject them in their entirety, and thus enter the terrible world of slogan-shouting and absolutist dogma, where reigns the unholy Trinity of Censorship, the Secret Police, and Death.

We need to keep our wits about us in the same way when we use metaphors like *the advance of civilization* or *the laws of physics*, or when a metaphor called *the business world* (otherwise known as *the private sector*) deals with metaphors like *production targets, parent companies* and *industrial action.* International negotiations are conducted for metaphorically named entities like *Great Britain,* or *the U.S.S.R.,* or *the U.S.A.* (otherwise known as *Uncle Sam*), or *New Zealand,* by metaphorically named entities like *Westminster,* or *the Kremlin,* or *the White House,* or that multiple metaphor *the Beehive.* Millions of people have given their lives for these metaphors, so there is no doubt of their importance; but substantial problems arise when we try to establish the exact nature of the tenors of which these names provide the vehicles. Even greater problems, perhaps, face us as we try to analyse into tenor and vehicle the central metaphors of the Christian, or indeed of any, religion; we mentioned two earlier, and could add other metaphors like *Father, Son, Spirit* (or *Breath* or *Wind*), *Heaven* (or *Sky*), *Rebirth, Redemption* and so on. Again, many have died, and killed, for these metaphors, often – sadly – in some attempt to prove that they are not metaphors at all. But how can the word *God* be anything other than the vehicle of a metaphor whose tenor remains, by definition, for ever beyond our grasp?

In the light of considerations like this we may well sympathize with the ambition to which Robert Frost confesses in the address we quoted earlier in this chapter:

> I have wanted in late years to go further and further in making metaphor the whole of thinking . . .

and with his claim about the importance – and indeed the sheer practicality – of the subject:

> What I am pointing out is that unless you are at home in the metaphor, unless you have had your proper poetical education in the metaphor, you are not safe anywhere. Because you are not at ease with figurative values: you don't know the metaphor in its strength and its weakness. You don't know how far you may expect to ride it and when it may break down with you. You are not safe in science: you are not safe in history.[8]

Ernest Fenollosa agrees and would take the matter a step further:

> Metaphor, the revealer of nature, is the very substance of poetry. The known interprets the obscure, the universe is alive with myth. The beauty and freedom of the observed world furnish a model, and life is pregnant with art. It is a mistake to suppose, with some philosophers of aesthetics, that art and poetry aim to deal with the general and the abstract. This misconception has been foisted upon us by mediaeval logic. Art and poetry deal with the concrete in nature, not with rows of separate "particulars", for such rows do not exist. Poetry is finer than prose because it gives us more concrete truth in the same compass of words. Metaphor, its chief device, is at once the substance of nature and of language.[9]

The universe is alive with myth. Every society that has ever inhabited the face of this planet has sought to provide itself with an identity, *a local habitation and a name,* by means of metaphor, and in particular by expanding metaphor into **myth**. Used thus, the word *myth* represents that series of extended metaphors which we perceive as embodying the truth more accurately and fully than anything else at our disposal. From the perspective of the twentieth century we view with some detachment, and perhaps nostalgia, the myths by which the ancient Greeks, Romans, Vikings and so on accounted for the world and their place in it. We re-explore, with endless fascination, those that similarly inform our own view of life: the great myth of progress that has shaped the western world since the sixteenth century, its daughter-myths like those of the American frontier and those that have crystallized since the mid-nineteenth century round the names of Charles

Darwin, Karl Marx and Sigmund Freud. And at the heart of our world picture remains the Judeo-Christian myth, endlessly reiterated and reinterpreted at all levels from the way we write today's date to the rigours of radical theology, and certainly the most capacious and powerful vehicle of human consciousness the world has ever seen.

Even such vehicles can get into the wrong hands, of course; and the more massive they are, the more damage they can cause when clumsily managed. We remain responsible for ourselves, and must not blame our metaphors for our own destructiveness:

> All metaphor breaks down somewhere. That is the beauty of it. It is touch and go with the metaphor, and until you have lived with it long enough you don't know when it is going. You don't know how much you can get out of it and when it will cease to yield. It is a very living thing. It is as life itself.[10]

Notes

1 Aristotle p. 78
2 harmonious dissonance
3 Johnson p. 678
4 Frost p. 217
5 Shakespeare *A Midsummer Night's Dream* V, i, 12-17
6 Fenollosa pp. 22-3
7 Fenollosa p. 24
8 Frost p. 219
9 Fenollosa p. 23
10 Frost p. 220

3

MEANING

We dance round in a ring and suppose;
But the Secret sits in the middle and knows.
Robert Frost

In this chapter we look at the question of what, and how, words mean. To do that, however, we need first to turn the question back to front and consider what we mean by *words*. Faced with a neatly printed page like this one we may not think that question too daunting. But all Scrabble players will begin to recognize some of its trickier dimensions: do things like *er, ouch, ahem, phew* and *hmph* qualify as words? And a little thought will take the problem even further: how do we classify ideograms like @, #, $, % and & — things that represent words or phrases without spelling out the sounds they make? And only a short step away from these wait the signs that warn us what to expect round the next bend of the road or help us find facilities at an airport.

Such perplexities all stem from a concept of *words* that we probably acquire as part of learning to read. Speech, after all, makes a continuous and generally unbroken noise — listen to any foreign-language radio station; and we acknowledge this when we write imitations of speech like *hasn't* and *shouldn't*. The gaps on the printed page that isolate what we call words function very much at random: why should we separate the negative prefix *not* while attaching the negative prefix *un* — we could as well write *she has notarrived* as *he is un welcome*. Latin and Greek inscriptions from classical times characteristically run all their letters together, disdaining any such factitious divisions. Our concept of *a word* probably results from the spread and development of writing and from scribal desire to achieve clarity or even simply avoid writer's cramp. The concept therefore rests on convention alone, and, like all matters of convention, remains prone to obscurity and subject to disagreement.

To realize this allows us to make some progress on the difference between

$ and *dollar(s)*, between *%* and per cent. Conventional visual differences should not blind us to obvious similarities in function. Most scholars get round the whole problem by preferring the term **symbol**, which covers both sorts nicely, to *word*, whose potential ambiguity somewhat disqualifies it. A further advantage of the term is that, without endorsing a fully realist theory of mimesis, it assumes that each word stands for something other than itself, something to which it *refers* which we can therefore call its **referent**. Having said which, in this chapter I shall stick to *word* as the more convenient term for the job in hand, which is to explore more fully what and how words mean, and to examine the relationship between symbol and referent as it affects us as writers.

When we want to know what any word means we normally turn to the dictionary, a document whose history and merits we will be discussing in the next chapter. Judges on the Bench, politicians in Parliament, students at the beginning of their essay all share the same respect for dictionaries and readiness to accept their pronouncements on the meanings of words. Why need we go further?

Charles Dickens faces this question, and suggests some interesting answers to it, in the course of his novel *Hard Times*. The relevant episode, worth quoting at some length, takes place in a Victorian schoolroom in the north of England:

"Girl number twenty," said Mr Gradgrind, squarely pointing with his square forefinger, "I don't know that girl. Who is that girl?"

"Sissy Jupe, Sir," explained number twenty, blushing, standing up, and curtseying.

"Sissy is not a name," said Mr Gradgrind. "Don't call yourself Sissy. Call yourself Cecilia."

"It's father as calls me Sissy, Sir," returned the young girl in a trembling voice, and with another curtsey.

"Then he has no business to do it," said Mr Gradgrind. "Tell him he mustn't. Cecilia Jupe. Let me see. What is your father?"

"He belongs to the horse-riding, if you please, Sir."

Mr Gradgrind frowned, and waved off the objectionable calling with his hand.

"We don't want to know anything about that, here. You mustn't tell us about that, here. Your father breaks horses, don't he?"

"If you please, Sir, when they can get any to break, they do break horses in the ring, Sir."

"You mustn't tell us about the ring, here. Very well, then. Describe your father as a horsebreaker. He doctors sick horses, I dare say?"

"Oh yes, Sir."

"Very well, then. He is a veterinary surgeon, a farrier, and horsebreaker. Give me your definition of a horse."

(Sissy Jupe thrown into the greatest alarm by this demand.)

"Girl number twenty unable to define a horse!" said Mr Gradgrind, for the general behoof of all the little pitchers. "Girl number twenty possessed of no facts, in reference to one of the commonest of animals! Some boy's definition of a horse. Bitzer, yours."

The square finger, moving here and there, lighted suddenly on Bitzer, perhaps because he chanced to sit in the same ray of sunshine which, darting in at one of the bare windows of the intensely whitewashed room, irradiated Sissy. For, the boys and girls sat on the face of the inclined plane in two compact bodies, divided up the centre by a narrow interval; and Sissy, being at the corner of a row on the sunny side, came in for the beginning of a sunbeam, of which Bitzer, being at the corner of a row on the other side, a few rows in advance, caught the end. But, whereas the girl was so dark-eyed and dark-haired, that she seemed to receive a deeper and more lustrous colour from the sun, when it shone upon her, the boy was so light-eyed and light-haired that the self-same rays appeared to draw out of him what little colour he ever possessed. His cold eyes would hardly have been eyes, but for the short ends of lashes which, by bringing themselves into immediate contrast with something paler than themselves, expressed their form. His short-cropped hair might have been a mere continuation of the sandy freckles on his forehead and face. His skin was so unwholesomely deficient in the natural tinge, that he looked as though, if he were cut, he would bleed white.

"Bitzer," said Thomas Gradgrind. "Your definition of a horse."

"Quadruped. Graminivorous. Forty teeth, namely, twenty-four grinders, four eye-teeth, and twelve incisive. Sheds coat in the spring; in marshy countries, sheds hoofs, too. Hoofs hard, but requiring to be shod with iron. Age known by marks in mouth." Thus (and much more) Bitzer.

"Now girl number twenty," said Mr Gradgrind. "You know what a horse is."[1]

In this passage Dickens deals with several of the issues that have occupied us in this book so far. The Benthamite utilitarian Gradgrind, ostensibly reducing the world to *facts* and numbers ("girl number twenty") ought to be a thoroughgoing 'realist', but betrays his unconscious and hypocritical nominalism when he tries to cope with disagreeable facts (such as circuses) by changing their names. And Dickens is clearly exploiting the metaphorical, indeed symbolic, potential of words like *square, sunbeam, light, dark* and *the intensely whitewashed room* in order to set his scene (the passage occurs early in the novel and introduces us to its heroine and villain). To reinforce what he is thus implying about language in general, Dickens raises the particular question of defining a horse: what does *horse* mean, and so, by extension, what do words mean? And *how* do they mean?

It becomes clear very quickly that dictionary definitions are not enough. The rote-learning of the rebarbative Bitzer makes a mockery of the question. And Dickens, to drive the point home, contrasts him with Sissy Jupe, who has spent her life with horses and *knows* about them in a way neither Bitzer nor Mr Gradgrind could begin to understand. That she cannot express what horses mean to her suggests not so much that she lacks the verbal equipment for the job; rather that the expression of such meaning lies beyond the capacity of words altogether. "Now, girl number twenty. You know what a horse is." How can words ever tell us what a horse, or a girl, or a classroom, or education, or hypocrisy, or anything, really *is*? So Dickens substantiates his own 'realism' as a novelist by exposing that of Mr Gradgrind for the sham that it is — but still, paradoxically, does it all by words! When it comes to conveying the meaning of anything, the dictionary definition comes at the bottom of the list; by trying to bypass the essential inaccuracy and ambiguity of language any definition actually confuses the issue, as anyone can tell who has had first hand experience of what it purports to be explaining. The very term *definition*, if you think about it, contradicts itself: language is not a *definite* medium, and we must look to the lies of poets and novelists — and of metaphor in general — for truth of any real value.

Part of the problem arises from the extreme ambiguity of the verb *to mean*. When we ask the questions "What does *horse* mean to Bitzer?" and "What does *horse* mean to Sissy?" we are probably asking questions of two different sorts. Their contexts — the separate experiences of the two children — force them apart: to Bitzer, *meaning* is a thing of the head, to be learnt from books, kept separate from experience and used as part of his manipulative approach to life; to Sissy, it is clearly a thing of the heart, inseparable from her emotions and bound up with her unaggressive and finally sacrificial personality.

We use the word *meaning* in both these senses — and in many others — all the time: if we speculate about the *meaning* of the word *rebarbative* as used a couple of paragraphs ago we probably begin by taking the Bitzerian line and looking it up in a dictionary; if, on the other hand, we ponder the *meaning* of the *Hard Times* passage as a whole we take account of its impact upon our emotions and come much nearer Sissy's approach. The phrase *you mean everything to me* takes this sense to its furthest extreme. And the word works in many other ways besides these two: 'this means war', 'he means no harm', and 'I mean to get to the bottom of this' convey shifting versions of another sense of the word. And there are several others: C. K. Ogden and I. A. Richards in their book *The Meaning of Meaning* isolate between sixteen and twenty-three different senses (the number depends on how they are grouped and shows, by its uncertainty, the complexity of the whole question: and if the term *meaning* is complex, the phrase *the meaning of meaning* must double, or perhaps square, that complexity).

We expect, therefore, no easy answers to questions about what a particular piece of language means. And as writers we need to bear in mind a whole range of variables in our efforts to control our meaning and convey it to our readers. From our comparison of Bitzer's and Sissy's assumptions emerges one possible distinction, that between **denotation** and **connotation**. It does not do to press this distinction too close, unless we are realists of the Gradgrind school; but it may suggest something useful about the way words work. Bitzer's concentration on the denotation of *horse* may arouse our suspicions about the category, while Sissy's bewilderment may confirm our fears and serve to redirect our attention to its connotations.

If a real world, separate from that which our language shapes, has any existence of its own, then these symbols that we call words have the job of (among other things) denoting something in that world, of depicting the *thing* that it is; and we can depict any *thing* in a variety of more or less efficient ways, by means either of the exact words or of others that do the same job nearly as well. And if we do not understand the exact words we can turn to those alternatives as explanatory substitutes. If you have read Chaper 1 of this book thoughtfully you will be aware of some of the holes in the theory of mimesis implied in these last few sentences, but in practice we often meet a new word and need to know what it means:

Little Robert: Mummy, what's tomorrow?
Mother: Tuesday, dear. Why?
Little Robert: No, I mean what's *tomorrow*?
Mother: I'm sorry, dear, I don't understand you.
Little Robert: Well, is *tomorrow* the day before today or the day after today?
Mother: Oh, I see what you mean! The day after today, dear.

The pregnant and laconic definitions which represent a parent's, and a lexicographer's, greatest challenge and triumph work towards a satisfactory statement of each word's denotation — 'the day after today', or a neat paraphrase of *rebarbative*, or the botanical classification of *rose*, perhaps. Not surprisingly, the most familiar words usually present the biggest problems of definition; they do their job so well that it seems redundant to find another set of terms to replace them. How would you define *horse*, for example? Or if you think Bitzer's effort incapable of improvement, try to concoct —

unaided and from scratch — a definition of *tree*. Old dictionary makers often shirked the task, either filching their predecessors' definitions or shying away from their responsibilities entirely: they were as likely to define *horse* as 'a beast in common use' as to produce the kind of thing quoted by Bitzer. Everyone, after all, knows what a horse is!

But do they, really? Does even Bitzer know? Or doesn't Sissy know a great deal better, inarticulate though she may be? Which is as much as to say that a word's denotation barely begins to explain what the word really means — and indeed, left to itself, may prove positively misleading. Around most words there cluster whole gatherings of connotations (though the metaphor implied in the words *around* and *cluster* in that statement may distort as much as it illuminates; is it really true to say that the word itself sits in the middle while its connotations somehow flit round the periphery?). All words bring to our experience of them the memories and experiences we connect them with, and the memories and experiences we connect with the *thing* we think the word denotes.

Some sets of connotations are widely shared. Words like *rose* and *lamb* appeal, for various reasons, to something like a communal consciousness among English-speaking peoples; most of us would identify and assent to the combination of transience and beauty implied by the first, and of innocence and edibility implied by the second. Again, the poets have had a lot to do with it; so has religion; and there may even be something in the objects themselves to reinforce the ideological tradition each has set so powerfully in motion. Roses at least smell nice — or used to. But beyond these shared connotations the words possess strong private associations for us all, consequent upon our private experiences of them: beyond a certain point, the sheep farmer is likely to respond to the word *lamb* very differently from the city dweller, and the Biblical scholar differently again from either. We all know what *tree* means, but J. R. R. Tolkien once confessed what a lot he had learnt about the word, and how much more it had come to mean to him as a result of writing the Entwood/Treebeard section of *The Lord of the Rings*.

Besides a word's denotation and connotations, we must take into account various other considerations (a jargonist would call them parameters) that shape its meaning. We never speak or write, to start with, from our full or entire personalities: each of us adopts a stance or **role** suited to the occasion. A letter to a grandparent or grandchild, for example, will require of us a different role from the one we adopt in a letter to an old school friend; and the personality we manifest in a job application will probably differ from the one we reveal in a letter of resignation. The difference this choice of role makes is of course obvious enough on the large scale: a carpenter using the word *vice* will unconsciously invest it with an entirely different denotation when switching roles and speaking as a moralist. Even *rose*, for all its power, will temporarily shift its meaning for a gardener assembling a watering-can. One word, this reminds us, can posssess two or more quite separate denotations: to describe something as *very dear*, without particularizing further, leaves our hearers uncertain whether we mean *beloved* or *expensive*. But we can equally effortlessly select the connotations of a word to suit our role of the moment: a careful reading of the little piece of dialogue we examined a page or two ago might detect a subtle change in what Mother means by the word *dear* as she changes roles from Helpful Mother to Baffled Mother and back again. Ponder for a moment the protean qualities of the word *writing*. If I announce a lecture or book on *writing*, my topic could be anything from *How To Produce A Novel* through *Calligraphy Made Plain* to *The History Of The Alphabet*. It will depend on my role, which will in turn become clearer as I define my topic.

What words mean therefore partly depends on what the writer intends them to mean. Modern literary criticism generally disapproves of speculating about the author's intention: 'stick to the words on the page', we are told, 'and don't go bothering about what you can never verify'. This may represent the right emphasis, and keep us from wandering into endless and unprofitable speculative byways; nevertheless we all habitually indulge in large and usually unconscious assumptions about the intentions of the authors we read. When Wordsworth writes:

> She lived unknown, and few could know
> When Lucy ceased to be:
> But she is in her grave, and, oh
> The difference to me!

we assume he intends the word *difference* to imply a sense of sadness and loss rather than one of hand-rubbing self-congratulation! Perhaps we should not dismiss *intention* altogether as an ingredient of meaning.

Our choice of role as writers will of course partly depend on the **audience** we perceive ourselves to be writing for; and the contribution of audience to word-meaning effectively complements that of role. We use words that suit our audience, and we monitor their connotations to avoid incongruity – unless under stress, in which case all sorts of things can go wrong. People reporting road accidents are particularly prone to this:

> I had been driving my car for forty years when I fell asleep at the wheel
> and had the accident.

The pedestrian had no idea which way to go so I ran over him.
The telephone pole was approaching fast. I was attempting to swerve out
of its path when it struck my front end.

Subjectivity runs riot in a crisis, which may explain why Wordsworth
preferred to write while recollecting his emotions in tranquillity. We laugh
to reassure ourselves of our sanity in resisting the distortions that the words
convey. By contrast the steward Malvolio, in Shakespeare's *Twelfth Night*,
renders his sanity suspect by imposing his own self-interested interpretation,
as audience, upon the Lady Olivia's words:

> Olivia: Maria, let this fellow be look'd to. . . . Let some of my people
> have a special care of him: I would not have him miscarry for the half of my
> dowry. [*Exeunt Olivia and Maria*]
> Malvolio: . . . "Let this fellow be look'd to:" fellow! not Malvolio, nor
> after my degree, but fellow.[2]

Generally, however, if we consider our audience and go halfway to meet
it we can reasonably expect it to cope with our meaning, even if it only
agrees to differ with us. The soldier on active service receiving a "Dear
John" letter hardly invests that word *dear* with any signification a dictionary
would recognize. Nor would his erstwhile girlfriend expect him to; her own
use of it has been ambiguous enough.

In the long run, the audience is probably going to impose its own view
anyway: if Malvolio had insisted long enough he would very likely have had
everyone around agreeing that *fellow* really meant *companion, equal* rather than
servant or *inferior*. The history of English abounds in words which have
gradually changed their meaning under some such pressure. As recently as
the eighteenth century *candid* (from Latin *candidus*, white) meant *kindly,
generous*. Two hundred years of people speaking candidly have changed all
that: 'whitewashing' is not the concern of the candid photographer. In the
same way *presently* has stopped meaning 'right away' and started to mean
'after some interval' (though North American usage may now be restoring
its old sense). In a particularly spectacular example of semantic shift, several
centuries of male chauvinism and dominance took the early Middle English
word *buhsum*, ('obedient, compliant,' from the Anglo-Saxon *buhan* 'to bow,
obey') and turned it into modern *buxom* with all that the term implies.
Words, for all their inaccuracy, sometimes have a nasty habit of telling the
truth, at least about those who use them.

The most important element in the relationship between writer and

The most important element in the relationship between writer and audience is **tone**, the term for whatever attitude we adopt towards our audience. An immense range of tones is of course available for our use – from the incantatory to the colloquial, the placatory to the aggressive, the candid (in any sense) to the ironic. This last is so important that we shall give it a chapter to itself; it is enough to say for the moment that an ironic tone will twist the meanings of our words very violently, as a glance at the passage from *Gulliver's Travels* discussed in Chapter 1 will show. Swift uses many words there in a sense diametrically opposite to anything we might expect under normal conditions; bad words come to mean good things and vice versa. But tone always limits and controls meaning: perhaps the solemn tone established in the Wordsworth poem we looked at above effectively inhibits us from any irresponsible reading of *difference* in the final line; no doubt to read the whole poem would increase this effect.

The sort of document we are writing will also bring influence to bear on the meaning of the words we use. We may call this **genre** or **format**. The phrase *Number 1 Best Seller* may have some independent meaning of its own; but when we see it on the cover of some work of pulp fiction we generally take it to mean *This is a work of pulp fiction* (why, by the way, are such works never the subject of *minor* films?) If we open such a book, and find that the first sentence reads "Lawrence wrote every day" we may reasonably assume that *Lawrence* is the hero's first name and that he spends a small portion of each day writing a love-letter. Meeting the very same sentence in a book of literary criticism, however, we would justifiably take *Lawrence* to be a surname (probably warranting the initials D. H. or T. E.) and the rest of the sentence a statement of that writer's compositional habits and daily routine between breakfast and dinner. Such is the power of genre that every element in that apparently simple four word declaration modifies its meaning according to its environment. Even the position of a word within a particular format affects its meaning. A wine label or wine list bestows a very special and particular meaning on the word *dry* – although small print at the bottom saying 'store in a cool *dry* place' restores that word to something more like its usual sense. And while I remain unmoved by the phrase *Dear Robert* at the top of letters from all sorts and conditions of people, its recurrence, even once, in the body of the communication would generate effects of quite a different kind.

When we write we usually consider ourselves to be writing about a particular **topic** which, we hope, suits the role and format we have chosen and the audience we have in mind. This too modifies and delimits word meaning. We saw earlier the effect of contextual subject-matter on a word under control. '*Dear* John' will know exactly what to make of the word as he reads on down his ex-girlfriend's letter and discovers the topic uppermost in her mind. And our attitude towards the topic – the **feeling**, in other words, which we generate in our writing – will play its part in regulating the meanings of our words as well. The possible range of feeling is of course as wide as the range of tone we discussed earlier in this chapter: both cover the entire world of human experience. We have all received letters from people trying to sound more cheerful than they feel, and have discovered what we take to be the real state of affairs by 'reading between the lines' – that is to say, by responding to connotations (of both vocabulary and phrasing) that the writer has not managed to control. The dismal phrase *just good friends* which any "Dear John" letter will almost certainly contain exemplifies the way feeling can establish meaning in defiance of normal denotations (though *unjust bad enemies* might be too cynical an expression of its real sense).

The four variables **Role**, **Audience**, **Format** and **Topic** (conveniently memorable by means of the acronym **RAFT**), together with their circumambient issues, thus all play their part in determining meaning and provide us as writers with some control over the meanings of the words and phrases we use. Certainly we will handle words more confidently if we identify the four before we begin writing and continue to pay some attention to them as we proceed through the various stages of the writing process. Of course they still oversimplify the whole enormously complicated business of meaning.

> Could mortal lip divine
> The undeveloped Freight
> Of a delivered syllable
> 'Twould crumble with the weight.[3]

What a word *means* (in all possible senses of that term) to me will represent the cumulative effect of all the hundreds or thousands of occasions on which I have met it, mediated by all the roles and audiences to which it has been geared and by all the formats and all the contextual topics that have influenced its impact on me; what it means to my reader will result from that reader's own personal set of experiences – and the circles of any two people's experiences will overlap only partially at the best of times. And that meaning will have grown, not on the pages of some dictionary or in the memory of any computer, but right here in my head, or right there in yours – though never identically on both. In Chapter 1 we touched upon John

Locke's insistence on this point in his *Essay Concerning Human Understanding*, where, using the discriminatory terminology and elaborate punctuation characteristic of the eighteenth century, he applies it to the writer's predicament thus:

> *Words* by long and familiar use, as has been said, come to excite in Men certain *Ideas*, so constantly and readily, that they are apt to suppose a natural connexion between them. But that they *signify* only Men's peculiar [i.e. individual] *Ideas* and that *by a perfectly arbitrary Imposition* is evident, in that they often fail to excite in others (even that use the same Language) the same *Ideas*, we take them to be the Signs of: And every Man has so inviolable a Liberty, to make Words stand for what *Ideas* he pleases, that no one hath the Power to make others have the same *Ideas* in their Minds, that he has, when they use the same Words, that he does. And therefore the great *Augustus* himself, in the Possession of that Power which ruled the World, acknowledged, he could not make a new Latin Word: which was as much as to say, that he could not arbitrarily appoint, what *Idea* any Sound should be a Sign of, in the Mouths and common Language of his Subjects.[4]

So Locke summarizes the writer's tragedy and triumph: all too often we *fail to excite in others* the ideas that seem so important or interesting to us; but if we succeed in spreading one new word with the new idea that it represents we can number ourselves among Shelley's "unacknowledged legislators of the world".

Most of us never progress much beyond the failure. Not only can we never tell the truth in words (if Chapter 1 is to be believed), but even if we could we would never be able to convey it to someone else. But unless, like Gulliver's sages, we are going to resign from language altogether, we have no option but to keep on trying, acknowledging the common humanity we share with our readers:

> Closely looked at, all novel-writing is a sort of shorthand. Even the most simple and broadly human situation cannot really be told in full. Each reader in following it unconsciously supplies a vast amount himself. A great deal of the effect is owing to things quite out of the picture given – things in the reader's own mind, first and foremost. The writer is playing on common experience; and mere suggestion is often far more effective than analysis. Take the paragraph in Turguénieff's 'Lisa' – it was pointed out to me by Henry James – where Lavretsky, on the point of marriage, after much suffering, with the innocent and noble girl whom he adores, suddenly hears that his intolerable first wife whom he had long believed dead is alive. Turguénieff, instead of setting out the situation in detail, throws himself on

the reader. 'It was dark. Lavretsky went into the garden, and walked up and down there till dawn.'

That is all. And it is enough. The reader who is not capable of sharing that night walk with Lavretsky, and entering into his thoughts, has read the novel to no purpose. He would not understand, though Lavretsky or his creator were to spend pages on explaining.[5]

Notes

1 Dickens Ch. II
2 Shakespeare *Twelfth Night* III, iv, 59ff.
3 Dickinson p.602
4 Locke p.408
5 Ward pp.230-1

4

CORRECTNESS AND 'THE DICTIONARY'

How forcible are right words!
but what doth your arguing reprove?
Job

Most of us, if asked to define good English, would probably give fairly high priority to formal correctness of some kind. In today's literate society, those who 'can't spell' feel themselves to be at a disadvantage, and we often hear people lamenting their lack of schooling in things like grammar and punctuation, or deploring the 'incorrectness' of someone else's (never their own) pronunciation. We all feel, that is to say, that correctness matters; but most of us, if pressed, would probably define it rather as an absence of incorrectness than as the presence of any positive quality – a bland and finally not very helpful definition.

As a start to a more constructive approach to the subject we will find it worthwhile to distinguish between the written and spoken forms of the language. This book must of course concentrate on the former, but we will do that better if we first acknowledge the enormous variety of ways in which people speak English in the late twentieth century – a far greater variety than any other language can boast. **Dialects** abound, representing all kinds of social, cultural, geographical and occupational divisions, sometimes spilling over those divisions to meet the needs of temporary and fluctuating groups, and in general facilitating the life, love, leisure and locomotion of the modern world. And within each dialect each speaker wields a personal and unique *idiolect* – a word-hoard and syntactical system not precisely duplicated, as Chapter 3 pointed out, by those of any other individual.

In Chapter 9 we shall glance briefly at the history and growth of English dialects. Here we must notice their changing status in the world's esteem during the last half-century or so. Today, few linguistic scholars would countenance the notion of any one dialect being more correct or 'pure' than any of the others; and scholarly attitudes are steadily and healthily infiltrating popular ones. Demonstrable reasons – cultural, economic, and just plain human – exist for the pre-eminence, during the last few centuries, of one particular dialect of English, but the better we understand those reasons the better we can dispute some of the conclusions they led to.

That dialect, spoken in the South-east Midlands of England – the triangle, very roughly, suspended between Oxford, Cambridge and London – became variously known as Oxford, the King's (or Queen's), B.B.C., or Received Standard English; fine-sounding names that still endow it, in some circles at any rate, with a reputation for correctness or desirability above that of its countless sibling dialects.

A hundred years or more of patience and good humour on the part of the speakers of other dialects, of political struggle for human equality, and of towering works of art like Mark Twain's novel *Huckleberry Finn* have been needed to put the South-east Midland dialect of English back into proper perspective – and indeed to restore to the poor thing the opportunities for growth and development which its formal and official status largely denied it for so long. No one, of course, who rates communication above status, or who has watched the struggles of any language learner to cope with the complex and delicate muscular movements demanded by *any* dialect, will readily rate one of them as absolutely 'better' than the others. In many ways, each of us is the sum of our language; to deny anyone's language is to deny that person's value or even existence, so that the injunction "Don't speak Maori (or Gaelic, or Basque, or Flemish) in the playground" amounts to something not far short of genocide. If therefore I dictate the way someone else talks I am laying claim to moral superiority over that person as a person and not merely as a speaker – playing God (while simultaneously demonstrating my unfitness for the role).

The written language, on the other hand, presents us with a different set of issues. Whatever dialect of English we may speak, the version we have all learnt to write rests very firmly upon South-east Midland speech. We may blame Geoffrey Chaucer, Dick Whittington, Archbishop Thomas Cranmer, William Shakespeare, King James I of England and VI of Scotland, John Bunyan, Samuel Johnson, Noah Webster, Sir James A. H. Murray and a host of others for this, but can do very little about it even if we wish to. It has cornered the market, so that when Robert Burns or Sir Walter Scott try to write Scottish English, or William Barnes tries to write Dorset, or Mark Twain imitates various dialects of the southern United States, they all produce standard South-east Midland English orthography heavily modified by variant spellings and peppered with apostrophes, every one of which bears mute testimony to the undimmed power and prestige of the system they are trying to modify. This brand of linguistic colonialism continues to pose enormous problems for the growing numbers of writers today who find South-east Midland increasingly distant from and irrelevant to their own dialects of English.

But written uniformity seems inevitable. In speech, whatever our differences, we can usually arrive at some kind of mutual understanding with the help of body language, gesture, intonation, repetition, explanation and even, if necessary, pictures. Some of these work even on voice-only devices like the telephone – though a wise South-east Midlander learns to say *tomayto* instead of *tomahto* on the phone in the U.S.A. (and no doubt vice versa). Writing, by contrast, relies for its effect on nothing but itself, and may indeed be read by many people other than those for whom we intend it in the first place. Few of us would care to compound the complexities of meaning examined in the previous chapter by dispensing with the conventional uniformity of the writing system we have inherited, whether it has grown from our own particular dialect or not.

Such uniformity has not always existed, but seems to have emerged in the wake of the printing-press and the spread of literacy. We should not exaggerate the variety that it replaced: clearly some conventions must always exist for written communication to happen at all, and each of the scriptoria that produced manuscripts before the advent of movable-type printing and the mass dissemination of literature had its own rules for spelling, punctuation, abbreviation and so on. But they were local rules, reflecting local tradition and dialect; and when copyists got hold of manuscripts written in a different dialect or according to the conventions of another scriptorium they usually transcribed them – often not very consistently – into their own, with sometimes bewildering results, especially after several transcriptions.

The printing press inevitably brought the dictionary in its wake. Manuscript copyists had first introduced the word lists or **glosses** from which our modern dictionaries ultimately derive. In the later Middle Ages, as the vernacular replaced Latin as the medium for scholarship and literature, scribes copying Latin manuscripts had found it convenient to list, in their margins, translations of the harder words; and they continued this habit as a means of explaining the unfamiliar words – from not only Latin but also Greek, French, Italian, Spanish and so on – that began to pour into English from the fifteenth century onwards. In due course separate lists of such words began to be collected into **glossaries**. Robert Cawdrey's *Table*

Alphabeticall, conteyning and teaching the true writing and understanding of hard usuall English words, borrowed from Hebrew, Greek, Latine and French etc, published in 1640, stands as perhaps the last and most sophisticated of these. As its title implies, alphabetical order had by no means gained a monopoly (arrangement by subject had been popular). Cawdrey concentrated on hard but current (*usuall*) words, and claimed authority on both their spelling and their meaning (*writing and understanding*).

In 1658, Edward Phillips expanded Cawdrey's work into *The New World of English Words* (the title again contains interesting overtones) which itself received the same treatment from John Kersey in 1706. These collectively paved the way for the true **dictionaries**, of which the first was Nathan Bailey's *An Universal Etymological Dictionary*, published in 1721. Bailey set out to list the entire English vocabulary rather than merely the difficult words, and – as his title suggests – to give some idea of where each word came from. Unfortunately each of the scholars just mentioned borrowed rather uncritically from his predecessor, with the result that much obsolete material and a growing number of errors (such as false etymologies) survived. The idea of 'the dictionary' was now firmly established, but needed someone of learning, industry and clear critical judgement to put it into effective operation. Dr Samuel Johnson (1709-84) possessed all these qualities in superabundance.

Johnson first published his monumental *Dictionary of the English Language* in 1755, having undertaken the research and composed the entries almost single-handed – a few copyists constituted his only assistance. He added illustrative quotations in support of his definitions. His personality and prejudices gleam from time to time through the impersonal scholarship at which he aimed, as when he defines *lexicographer* as "A writer of dictionaries, a harmless drudge, that busies himself in tracing the original, and detailing the signification of words", or *oats* as "A grain, which in England is generally given to horses, but in Scotland supports the people". His definition of *network* is equally famous, though for different reasons: "Any thing reticulated or decussated, at equal distances, with intersections between the interstices" (*to decussate*, Johnson tells us elsewhere, means to "intersect at acute angles". The entry under *patron* hints at the hardships and bitterness of his scholarly and literary struggles. "One who countenances, supports, or protects. Commonly a wretch who supports with insolence, and is paid with flattery."

Johnson lived at a time when, after the turbulence of the previous century, people wanted settled ways of doing things not only in politics but in every aspect of life – not least in the vocabulary and syntax by means of which they shaped their world. Johnson's *Dictionary* gave form and authority to a system of conventions largely still current today, went into many editions over many decades, and in due course stimulated Noah Webster's *Compendious Dictionary of the English Language*, first published in 1828 and designed to give American usage similar authoritative sanction. Webster's *Dictionary* in its turn provoked further lexicographical effort in Britain, culminating in the great *Oxford English Dictionary* begun in 1878 under the editorship of Sir James A. H. Murray and eventually completed in 1933.

Both *Webster* and *O.E.D.* have regularly been updated, and most modern desk or pocket dictionaries stand heavily indebted to one or both – an exception being the recently issued *Collins COBUILD English Language Dictionary* which, serving students of English as a second language, has used computer analysis to select its words from current written materials and introduced definitions of a less formal kind than that inherited from Johnson. Specialist dictionaries continue to flourish, sustaining the tradition of the 'hard word list'.

Most lexicographers today, however, wear their cloak of authority with some embarrassment, claiming to record how the language *is* used rather than how it *should be* used – seeing their function, that is to say, as descriptive rather than prescriptive. Our brief historical survey of dictionaries should encourage us to remember that most represent the opinions and findings of a mere handful of individuals whose work goes out of date even before it leaves the printing-press. Most lexicographers would welcome and encourage such scepticism. But 'the dictionary' (as most of us revealingly persist in calling it) continues in general to exercise an almost mesmeric authority ultimately deriving from Johnson's personal prestige and the climate of opinion he wrote in.

His attitude to correctness becomes clear in the opening paragraphs of the *Preface* he wrote for his *Dictionary*:

It is the fate of those who toil at the lower employments of life to be rather driven by the fear of evil than attracted by the prospect of good; to be exposed to censure, without hope of praise; to be disgraced by miscarriage, or punished for neglect, where success would have been without applause, and diligence without reward.

Among these unhappy mortals is the writer of dictionaries; whom mankind have considered not as the pupil, but the slave of science, the pioneer of literature, doomed only to remove rubbish and clear obstructions from the paths through which Learning and Genius press forward to conquest and glory, without bestowing a smile on the humble drudge that facilitates their progress. Every other author may aspire to praise; the lexicographer can only hope to escape reproach, and even this negative recompense has been yet granted to very few.

I have, notwithstanding this discouragement, attempted a dictionary of the English language, which, while it was employed in the cultivation of every species of literature, has itself been hitherto neglected; suffered to spread, under the direction of chance, into wild exuberance, resigned to the tyranny of time and fashion, and exposed to the corruptions of ignorance, and caprices of innovation.

When I took the first survey of my undertaking, I found our speech copious without order, and energetic without rules: wherever I turned my view, there was perplexity to be disentangled, and confusion to be regulated; choice was to be made out of boundless variety, without any established principle of selection; adulterations were to be detected, without a settled test of purity, and modes of expression to be rejected or received, without the suffrages of any writers of classical reputation or acknowledged authority.

Having therefore no assistance but from general grammar, I applied myself to the perusal of our writers; and noting whatever might be of use to ascertain or illustrate any word or phrase, accumulated in time the materials of a dictionary, which, by degrees, I reduced to method, establishing to myself, in the progress of the work, such rules as experience and analogy suggested to me; experience, which practice and observation were continually increasing; and analogy, which, though in some words obscure, was evident in others.

In adjusting the ORTHOGRAPHY, which has been to this time unsettled and fortuitous, I found it necessary to distinguish those irregularities that are inherent in our tongue, and perhaps coeval with it, from others which the ignorance or negligence of later writers has produced. Every language has its anomalies, which, though inconvenient, and in themselves once unnecessary, must be tolerated among the imperfections of human things, and which require only to be registered, that they may not be increased, and ascertained, that they may not be confounded: but every language has likewise its improprieties and absurdities, which it is the duty of the lexicographer to correct or proscribe.[1]

Johnson has thus far made little distinction between spoken and written language; indeed in his fourth paragraph he moves from *our speech* to the authority of *writers* without showing any awareness of inconsistency. No doubt by *our speech* he means the South-east Midland dialect, whose reputation for superiority must therefore already have been well established (though Johnson had the magnanimity once to give his biographer James Boswell, a Scot, the dubious reassurance "Sir, your pronunciation is not offensive"). When he does acknowledge the distinction between written and spoken language he seems to give priority to the written form, seeing pre-literary speech as a "wild and barbarous jargon", and literature as corrective linguistic therapy – a view that would find few adherents among scholars today:

> As language was at its beginning merely oral, all words of necessary or common use were spoken before they were written; and while they were unfixed by any visible signs, must have been spoken with great diversity, as we now observe those who cannot read to catch sounds imperfectly, and utter them negligently. When this wild and barbarous jargon was first reduced to an alphabet, every penman endeavoured to express, as he could, the sounds which he was accustomed to pronounce or to receive, and vitiated in writing such words as were already vitiated in speech. The powers of the letters, when they were applied to a new language, must have been vague and unsettled, and, therefore, different hands would exhibit the same sounds by different combinations.
>
> From this uncertain pronunciation arise, in a great part, the various dialects of the same country, which will always be observed to grow fewer and less different, as books are multiplied; and from this arbitrary representation of sounds by letters proceeds that diversity of spelling, observable in the Saxon remains, and, I suppose, in the first books of every nation, which perplexes or destroys analogy, and produces anomalous formations that being once incorporated can never be afterwards dismissed or reformed . . .[2]

Johnson's shrewd remarks on the problems of writing down a 'new language' cast light on the difficulties that must have faced those who undertook to adapt the Roman alphabet to hitherto unwritten languages like, for example, Maori in nineteenth century New Zealand. Other points worth noting include the twin criteria, *experience* and *analogy*, by which Johnson tries to systematize linguistic forms and which at the same time keep his own legislative instincts within bounds; he seeks the *rules, regulations, principles, purity* and *method* so dear to the eighteenth century mind (each of those terms makes a rewarding study in its political, social, moral and theological as well as linguistic senses), and claims a far more prescriptive role for lexicography in *correcting* or *proscribing improprieties and absurdities* than would most of his modern successors; but he nevertheless retains a healthy and realistic sense of the limits of such an authoritarian approach, and manifests the *tolerance* which *experience* must always entail.

We may assess the contribution of Johnson and his contemporary linguistic legislators by examining some of their judgements. As befitted an age that saw the birth of the Royal Society, they turned to the analogy between mathematical and verbal languages in order to rationalize the use of the negative. To Chaucer, in the fourteenth century, negatives reinforce each other. In the portrait of his Knight we learn that:

> He nevere yet no vileynye ne sayde
> In al his lyf unto no maner wight.[3]

"Nevere . . . no . . . ne . . . no" provide us with fourfold assurance of the absence of discourtesy (*vileynye*) in the Knight's speech to any sort of person (*maner wight*). To mathematicians on the other hand two negatives make a positive, so that *not none* means *some*, and the vulgar *there ain't nobody here* becomes proscribed. *Ain't* itself lost support in favour of *aren't*, while *you was* gave place to *you were*. All these had been widely used by speakers of all classes well into the eighteenth century, and all have flourished since then in that South-east Midland sub-dialect known as cockney and attributed until recently to speakers of a less educated and sophisticated kind.

Such legislation not only thus reinforces class distinction but also widens the gap between written and spoken usages. The eighteenth century insistence (based on Latin grammar) that 'the verb *to be* takes no object' generates *it is I, it was he* and underlies utterances like that in *The Jackdaw of Rheims* where

> heedless of grammar, they all cried, "THAT'S HIM!"

But "Be thou me!" cries the poet Shelley to his skylark, where "Be thou I" would be unthinkable. The tension between writing and speech remains, though in the twentieth century scholarly attention has refocused on the spoken language, with the written form consequently losing much of the prestige with which Johnson endowed it. Only recently have scholars begun to acknowledge its separate and independent importance.

Nevertheless, written English continues to derive many advantages from the regulations of Johnson and his era. Learners of English may deplore the range of sounds represented by the *-ough* spelling (*though, through, thorough, bough, cough, rough* and so on) but many of these contribute usefully to distinctions in meaning; it helps us as readers to be able to tell *bough* from *bow*, *through* from *threw*, and even *rough* from *ruff*. We have comparatively few sounds at our disposal in speech, and consequently need to re-use them for different purposes. Misunderstanding can, and does, result: we can mis-hear *wait* for *weight*, *ate* for *eight*, *sure* for *shore*, *morning* for *mourning*, *thyme* for *time*, *discreet* for *discrete*, *born* for *borne* (or *bourne*), *heir* for *air*, *pear* for *pair* (or *pare*), *compliment* for *complement* and so on and so on. Differences in spelling give writing a considerable edge over speech in this respect; indeed we frequently clarify our spoken words by spelling them for our hearers, and ought to thank Johnson and the lexicographers for the ability to do so.

We ought perhaps also to ponder the consequences that would follow the implementation – assuming such a thing to be possible – of any proposal for the reform and simplification of our spelling system. For most of us, a word's spelling rates as part of its meaning and impact. Most people spell *connection* thus; I spell it – when I can remember to do so – *connexion*, in order to show my solidarity with Jane Austen and *The Times* newspaper and to reassure myself that I'm distinguishable from 'most people'. It is only the accepted spelling of *civilization* that enables Mark Twain to make his point by having Huck Finn spell it *sivilization*, or e.e cummings to take it one stage further as *siphilization*. Rebels are only rebels if they have something to rebel against. And to anyone proposing that English should be spelt as pronounced we should immediately put the question *Pronounced by whom?* – the inhabitants of London (East or West Ends?), of Oxford (Town or Gown?), of Glasgow, of Boston, of New Orleans (black or white?), of Cape Town (ditto) or of Sydney? And these all speak with near uniformity when compared with multitudes of speakers of English in some of its Pidgin or Creole forms.

In much the same way, the complex and sophisticated system of punctuation which the eighteenth century also ratified invests writing with meanings which speech finds it hard to duplicate – though Victor Borge does his best. Capital (upper case) letters convey much, as we acknowledge when we distinguish *God* from *god*, or as poet e. e cummings acknowledges when he largely abandons their use, writing in the first person *i* rather than *I*; in one of his poems only Women achieve the dubious eminence. Quotation marks, single or double (' ' or " "), besides enclosing direct 'speech', enable a writer to convey a variety of cautions, doubts or ironies for the reader's benefit, as I have just done with " 'speech'." *Italics* (or their manuscript equivalent <u>underlining</u>), as well as imparting emphasis, provide a handy alternative to quotation marks as a way of isolating words from their grammatical context; I use them thus in this paragraph and throughout this book. Such things become tricky to convey when read aloud, and can easily get lost or even pose dangers: "*Emma* reaches a climax at Box Hill" offers, as written, a tolerable suggestion about the structure of Jane Austen's novel; but we need the italics. Punctuation marks like the semi-colon (;) and colon (:) each make their unique contribution to the meaning of what we write: the semi-colon suggests a continuity of theme between the two sentences it separates, or at least some common quality among the items of the list it punctuates; while the colon implies something even more powerful by way of equivalence or consequence in the sentence that follows it. Mark Twain, arriving in England at the height of his fame to give a series of lectures, objected to the punctuation of a newspaper hoarding:

Mark Twain Arrives: Ascot Cup Stolen

Perhaps the humble and apparently inoffensive comma wields more power than any other punctuation mark. The insertion of two can turn a sentence like "Police officers open to bribery pervert the course of justice" into matter for a libel suit; and a doctor writing "However the patient feels she is unlikely to recover" must put a comma somewhere to make sense. Where it goes, however, separates life from death.

All this may suggest several conclusions about the problems of correctness we raised at the start of this chapter. Clearly, no absolute standards of linguistic right and wrong exist, much as we might like them to, or dearly as we would like to enshrine the precepts we received from our parents or the principles we found in the world around us when we reached the age of about fourteen. Language, as we shall see in Chapter 9, changes too relentlessly – as does the world it reflects – for such permanency to be possible. Equally clearly, we can assess the correctness of a piece of language only in the context of the world around it as well as of the RAFT of variables we examined in Chapter 3. It would be wrong for Huck Finn to talk like an Oxford undergraduate (though I have known Oxford undergraduates who talked like Huck Finn).

Perhaps in the end the term *correctness* misleads us, and we should substitute some word like *convention*. All communication depends on shared conventions, and written English, as we have seen, possesses a wide and subtle range of them. Learning to write means, for the most part, learning to handle conventions of one sort or another – conventions which, once under our control, we can ignore or contravene just as freely as we can follow them: in either case we acknowledge them, just as do those who try to reproduce dialects other than the South-east Midland in their writing. These conventions, moreover, matter more on some occasions than on others: when my daughter, in a letter home, spells *yesturday* thus (presumably by analogy, in the best Johnsonian manner, with *Saturday*) I cheerfully accept it as part of her role as the affectionate daughter of a university lecturer in English. But the same solecism in a letter of application for a job will probably invalidate the whole thing; we live under the same obligation to spell such documents 'correctly' as we do to avoid wearing holed T-shirt and frayed jeans at the job interview. It is simply the way the world works; we may not like it, but can do very little about it.

Other kinds of correctness should even provoke our active resistance. To people of totalitarian inclination a text's political, moral or theological correctness may take precedence over all other criteria, and the Censor replace the dictionary as the final authority. Whatever the arguable benefits of censorship, dictating the thinking of others must entail even greater dangers (to the censor as well as to the censored) than curtailing or 'correcting' their speech in the fashion we mentioned earlier – and for much the same reasons. No human agency ought to possess such horrifying power, as John Milton implies in his eloquent plea against censorship, addressed to the seventeenth century British Parliament:

> Truth indeed came once into the world with her divine Master, and was a perfect shape most glorious to look on: but when he ascended, and his Apostles after him were laid asleep, then strait arose a wicked race of deceivers, who as that story goes of the *Ægyptian Typhon* with his conspirators, how they dealt with the good *Osiris*, took the virgin Truth, hewd her lovely form into a thousand peeces, and scatter'd them to the four winds. From that time ever since, the sad friends of Truth, such as durst appear, imitating the careful search that *Isis* made for the mangl'd body of *Osiris*, went up and down gathering limb by limb still as they could find them. We have not yet found them all, Lords and Commons, nor ever shall doe, till her Master's second comming; he shall bring together every joynt and member, and shall mould them into an immortall feature of lovelines and perfection. Suffer not these licencing prohibitions to stand at every place of opportunity forbidding and disturbing them that continue seeking, that continue to do our obsequies to the torn body of our martyr'd Saint.[4]

Perhaps a censorship-free society merits the judgement Winston Churchill once applied to democracy: "the worst system in the world, except for all the others."

Our irrepressible respect for 'correctness' probably recognizes in somewhat limited guise that ideal for which all responsible writers strive in one way or another. We all want, in the end, to get our product right, to produce either good prose – according to Coleridge's definition "words in their best order " – or good poetry, "the best words in the best order". But to achieve this takes a great deal more than a dictionary and a handbook of grammar, indispensable as these may be. And which of us would ever claim fully to have achieved it anyway? For most writers, including even the very greatest:

>   . . . every attempt
> Is a wholly new start, and a different kind of failure
> Because one has only learnt to get the better of words
> For the thing one no longer has to say, or the way in which
> One is no longer disposed to say it[5]

Writing, an art as well as a craft, demands both inspiration and perspiration, each fertilizing the other. Neither produces worthwhile offspring in isolation: the profoundest insights die aborning unless fleshed in verbal symbols, with the conventions of language in attendance as midwives to establish them in the world; while a slavish subservience to 'the rules' generates a barren formalism, a mere waxwork rather than a breathing human spirit. "Look in thy heart and write" says Sir Philip Sidney, but he says so in the last line of a sonnet, that most elaborately designed and crafted form of writing.[6] Mary Augusta Ward (Mrs Humphry Ward) finds something of the same challenge confronting her as a novelist in the nineteenth century:

> There are five and twenty ways
> Of constructing tribal lays –
> And every single one of them is right!

– always supposing that the way chosen quickens the breath and stirs the heart of those who listen. But when the subject chosen has two aspects, the one intellectual and logical, the other poetic and emotional, the difficulty of holding the balance between them so that neither overpowers the other, and interest is maintained, is admittedly great.[7]

Correctness in writing, that is to say, stems from and demands balance, tact, alertness and compromise. T. S. Eliot both preaches and practises this conclusion when he characterizes "every phrase And sentence that is right" as a place where:

>   every word is at home,
> Taking its place to support the others,
> The word neither diffident nor ostentatious,
> An easy commerce of the old and the new,
> The common word exact without vulgarity,
> The formal word precise but not pedantic,
> The complete consort dancing together[8]

Notes

1 Johnson pp. 307-8
2 ibid.
3 Chaucer p. 124 *The Canterbury Tales I* (A) 70-71
4 Milton Vol II pp. 549-50
5 Eliot p. 16
6 Sidney, Sir Philip *Loving in truth*
7 Ward p. 230
8 Eliot p. 38

5

IRONY AND AMBIGUITY

Thank you for sending me your manuscript. I shall lose
no time in reading it.

attributed to *Benjamin Disraeli*

The word **irony** and its history return us to some of the interesting and
problematical questions of meaning we examined in Chapters 1 and 3.
Derived from a Greek term suggesting deception or evasiveness, the word
(or symbol) emerged in the sixteenth century and began to acquire its
current sense as late as the eighteenth. Since then it has broadened to cover
an increasing variety of literary and other phenomena, and today forms an
indispensable part of any reader's or critic's equipment for examining and
comparing certain experiences many people deem of central importance to
their understanding of the world.

We may well wonder how major ironists like Chaucer and Donne got on
without the word before the eighteenth century. Both seem to have used,
and presumably observed, the *thing* – or if they didn't, we need
fundamentally to change the way we respond to them today. Chaucer's
immediate successors praised him mainly for elaborate rhetorical
adornments which, if the modern reader notices them at all, seem of little
relevance or appeal; fifteenth century commentators certainly betrayed no
awareness of the ironic qualities in his writing that strike us so forcibly
today. Even as late as the eighteenth century, critics like Dr Johnson reading
the poetry of Donne and his fellow metaphysicals responded mainly to their
ingenuity, versification and *wit*.[1] Whether we assume that such people failed
to talk about irony merely because they lacked the vocabulary in which to
do so, or whether we conclude, on the other hand, that the absence of the
word incapacitated them from experiencing the *thing* depends on our
priorities and our attitudes to the kind of mimetic issues we saw George
Orwell and Northrop Frye debating in Chapter 1. The whole question, if
pursued, will lead us into the tortuous paths of contemporary speculation

about writer, text and audience – how much the writer contributes to a given piece of writing, how much is 'really' there in it, and how much, by contrast, the reader brings to it; or how far our responses are limited by the terminology available to us, and how far we fail to see what is under our noses for want of the words to illuminate it.

Not that any word vouchsafes the full content of its meaning straight away – least of all a complex term like *irony*, whose arrival two hundred years ago prompted what promises to be an unending series of attempts to define it – to describe the reality (if we adopt Orwell's position) of which it acts as a symbol, and to disclose further examples of its hitherto covert operations in various corners of the world of human experience; or (if we agree with Frye) to add something more to the cumulative processes of thought and thus to expand human consciousness a little further. Of the making of books on irony there appears to be no end. Some twentieth century critics have even suggested that the tension or equilibrium generated by irony forms an essential ingredient of great poetry and indeed gives us a useful yardstick by which to measure its superiority over other, 'one-dimensional,' writing. Others, more recently still, have wondered whether our concern with irony reveals more about us than about the literature we read, and whether it will prove in the end to be just another passing fashion like the obsession with rhetoric in the middle ages or the passion for the sublime in the eighteenth century.

Be this as it may, we recognize the presence of irony when some incongruity or discrepancy occurs between what appears to be and what actually is. Thus defined, it can occur in a wide variety of ways, non-verbal as well as verbal. Some have seen it as an animating principle of the universe we live in; things indeed are not always what they seem, and this notion of **cosmic irony** may help us to make some kind of sense of our often baffling human predicament. Its more pessimistic version surfaces at moments like that at the end of Kingsley Amis's novel *The Anti-Death League,* where a sceptical clergyman enjoys his first real conviction of God's goodness just before a lorry kills his beloved dog outside the church. But the idea is not entirely incompatible with religious faith and the Judaeo-Christian tradition, as a study of the story of Jacob or the Book of Jonah in the Old Testament will show. A loving God may also be – indeed must be, if you look at the world – an ironist of some kind or other.

But the affectionate and accepting kind of irony that emerges in works like the Book of Jonah, the plays of Sophocles and the poetry of Chaucer contrasts strongly with the more bitter and desperate kind implied by Amis and explored by Greek tragedians like Aeschylus and Euripides and by

English writers like Thomas Hardy and Jonathan Swift. This distinction between *affirmative* and *destructive* irony seems common to all its manifestations, and may well in the end rate as more important than the subdivisions we may observe between various types.

One frequently recognized type, **structural irony**, exploits the discrepancy that occurs when we feel ourselves attracted to the hero or narrator of a story but realize at the same time that he or she is naive, fallible or even a fool. Its immediate effect, of course, is to make us recognize similar dubious qualities in ourselves and question the soundness of our own judgements; and it works the more powerfully if we have previously allowed ourselves to be tempted into uncritical satisfaction with our own insight and perceptiveness. This kind of irony sits at the heart of much of Chaucer's poetry and acts as the driving principle behind such narrators as Swift's Gulliver or Mark Twain's Huckleberry Finn.

Romantic irony exploits while in some ways inverting this approach to structure, emerging at moments when authors acknowledge their fictions for what they are and temporarily destroy narrative illusion by communicating directly with their audience:

> There's only one slight difference between
>   Me and my epic brethren gone before,
> And here the advantage is my own, I ween
>   (Not that I have not several merits more,
> But this will more peculiarly be seen);
>   They so embellish, that 'tis quite a bore
> Their labyrinth of fables to thread through,
> Whereas this story's actually true.
>
> If any person doubt it, I appeal
>   To history, tradition and to facts,
> To newspapers, whose truth all know and feel,
>   To plays in five, and operas in three acts;
> All these confirm my statement a good deal,
>   But that which more completely faith exacts
> Is, that myself, and several now in Seville,
> *Saw* Juan's last elopement with the devil.[2]

Byron here deliberately casts ironic doubt on the veracity not of his hero (and still less of himself as narrator) but of the very substance of his story.

The stage provides such a rich medium for the culture of structural irony that it has acquired its own special version, **dramatic irony**. This characteristically occurs when a dramatist allows the audience information withheld from one or more of the characters in the play: we know that Desdemona is innocent, or that Godot will never come, and have to look on under some stress as Othello or Vladimir and Estragon suspect or hope otherwise. "A little water clears us of this deed" says Lady Macbeth, red-handed with the murder of Duncan and his grooms, little knowing (as we do) that in her agony later she will exclaim "Here's the smell of the blood still: all the perfumes of Arabia will not sweeten this little hand." Again, our judgement and sympathy run counter to each other and we learn more about ourselves and our true values as a result.

Another type, **Socratic irony**, enshrines Socrates' habitual – and highly successful – educational technique of asking a series of apparently naive and easily answerable questions leading inexorably to a conclusion none but he could foresee. This is the earliest sense in which the word *irony* occurred in English, and seems to have spawned all the rest. Feigned ignorance remains a valuable pedagogic tool, since the lesson, self-taught, remains far more firmly implanted in the mind of the learner than if it had merely been imposed from outside.

All the foregoing, though most conveniently illustrated from literature of one sort or another, represent forms of irony that we may well encounter in our own experience, largely unmediated by language, and that we may therefore describe as **situational irony**. This often entails some measure of ignorance on someone's part – whether it be Sohrab and Rustum fighting to the death unaware, until too late, that they are son and father, or whether it be me cooking with salt under the impression that it is castor sugar. But ignorance does not seem to be an essential ingredient of an ironic situation, and perhaps the keenest irony occurs when the participants, fully alive to the ironic discrepancy, are still unable to disentangle themselves from it. In Corneille's classical French tragedy *Le Cid* heroic duty and love ironically reinforce each other as the heroine, Chimène, recognizes that she and her lover Don Rodrigue can each show themselves morally worthy of the other only by nobly prosecuting the vendetta between their families:

> Tu t'es, en m'offensant, montré digne de moi;
> Je me dois, par ta mort, montrer digne de toi.[3]

"You, by causing me offence [he has killed her father] have shown yourself worthy of me; by your death I must show myself worthy of you". Not far short of cosmic in its impact, this demonstrates the potential for irony latent within any highly regulated social or moral system.

Our more immediate concern as writers, however, must be **verbal irony**.

This may be defined as 'saying one thing and meaning another' or 'words that imply something different from what they purport to say'. Language therefore must, in one sense, generate irony all the time because of the gap we examined in the earlier chapters of this book between a word and its referent, between language and any reality it attempts to imitate or represent. If a word *means* something other than itself then there must remain some discrepancy between the two, and discrepancy breeds irony. This sounds like a local manifestation of the universal or cosmic irony we discussed above, but since we habitually use a lot of language without consciousness of irony we must also ask again whether irony, like the noise made by a tree falling in an uninhabited jungle, can be credited with any real existence in the absence of anyone to experience it.

Perhaps a better term for this perennial condition of language is **ambiguity**, a quality to which as writers we should remain alert at all times, asking ourselves:

> whether a sentence is ambiguous; whether it really means more than one thing or more than the writer intended; whether it can be so read as to mean something different.

or

> whether there is something clear on paper, but ambiguous if spoken aloud.[4]

This is not to suggest that we can, or indeed always should, avoid ambiguity. It sits at the heart of puns, of course – some of which can be very good indeed (to a woman who once asked him what he took to be the chief difference between the sexes Oscar Wilde replied, "Madam, I cannot conceive"). And it provides the basis for the two most effective ways that humanity possesses of conveying the truth in words – metaphor and irony, both of which attempt that daunting task by telling a lie and leaving the audience to penetrate to the truth for themselves; again, the self-taught lesson works best. Most imaginative literature, and all poetry, exploit or even celebrate language's enduring and exhilarating uncertainty. But avoidable ambiguity can hinder communication, so that if New Zealanders invite English guests to *tea* or *supper*, both parties do well to clarify when the meal will be served and what it will consist of.

Thus to identify and place ambiguity will also help us towards a more accurate and helpful appreciation of verbal irony. If the English guests turn up for *tea* at 3.30pm expecting Earl Grey and cucumber sandwiches they may find themselves in the midst of an ironic situation, but the word *tea* itself remains innocent of ironic tinge. Such commonplace ambiguity lacks the edge or bite, the wry sensation (whether it be smile, shrug, shudder or curl of the lip) by which we know the presence of irony, and by means of which we must in part define it. This sensation also remains the most difficult aspect of irony to explain. Most of us have probably, at one time or another, undertaken the hopeless task of trying to explain a piece or irony to some literalist incapable, by reason of age or temperament, of grasping it. We might as well have saved our breath. Even so, the heaviest calibre of verbal irony, **sarcasm**, may penetrate the thickest hide, and on the more vulnerable can inflict considerable pain:

> Sticks and stones
> May break my bones,
> *And* words can *often* hurt me.

We may now usefully turn to some examples of irony in action in order to explore some of its lineaments and complexities. Some time in the late nineteenth century the British comic magazine *Punch* published a cartoon depicting three young persons over the following caption:

> First youth: Hullo, congenital idiot!
> Second youth: Hullo, you priceless old ass!
> The damsel: I'd no idea you two knew each other so well.

This, though a slight foundation on which to build a study of irony, offers some interesting suggestions. In the first place, each of the youths is being ironic, at a fairly simple level, at the other's expense. Neither, presumably, would stand by the denotions of the words he uses; perhaps neither is of the sort to realize that his words possess anything by way of clear denotation at all. We, the audience, however, know all about the meaning of *idiot* and *ass* so the necessary ironic discrepancy exists somewhere – which suggests the important point that irony by no means depends on the intention of the person uttering the ironic words: something uttered in all honesty and simplicity may nevertheless make indisputable ironic impact on its audience. The letter to the newspaper that says "I approve of capital punishment for murderers because killing people in any circumstances is utterly abhorrent" generates the more irony because of the writer's unawareness of it.

But the point of the *Punch* cartoon presumably lies not in the youths' rather fatuous greetings but in the damsel's irony in pretending to take them literally. And, we may think, serve them right! She casts them, that is to say, as victims or **alazons** of her irony. Students of irony use this term (pronounced *a lad's on*) to identify anyone whose inadequacy a piece of irony exposes. The word comes from a Greek term for a boaster or braggart, and reminds us that one of the central functions of irony is to divide the world into two camps – *them* and *us*: *they* are the fools, the people who don't measure up, the victims at whose expense *we* amuse ourselves and in relation to whom *we* reassure ourselves about our own normality and superiority (wonderful combination!). Irony in this way makes an immediate appeal to one of the deepest – though not perhaps one of the most admirable – impulses known to the human race. To take the joke in this way enrols us into a mutual admiration society with the damsel.

But further thought may suggest another possible reading. The damsel may be responding quite seriously to the youths' greetings, fully as imperceptive as they to the denotations of their words. In this case the joke is on her as much as on them and she joins them as alazon, victim of our superior perceptions as readers aware (unlike her) of the silliness of late Victorian – and much other – slang. The drawing of the cartoon may or may not have suggested how naive she is. But the longer we explore this possibility the harder it becomes to tell where the truth lies and the more we realise the ambiguity of the damsel's words. And we then have to face the realization that our uncertainty makes it possible that the cartoonist is in some quiet way laughing at *us* for our ill-founded and short-lived assumption of superior insight, and we join the damsel, no longer as ironists but as alazons in our turn – and serve *us* right! Even though the cartoonist may have had no intention to do all this, it has somehow happened; we have again encountered the fundamental ambiguity of language. And once we admit ambiguity, and diagnose its effect as ironic, we run the permanent risk of being served with our own summonses and facing our own judgements:

> Judge not, that ye be not judged. For with what judgement ye judge, ye shall be judged: and with what measure ye mete, it shall be measured to you again[5]

voices one of the profoundest and most inescapable truths in the world.

This may all sound a large conclusion to draw from one Victorian joke. It nevertheless provides good evidence of the proneness of language to ambiguity, and of how quickly the semantic ice starts to give way when we try to put any weight on it. And it faintly echoes the kind of thing achieved systematically and brilliantly by some of the great English ironists – people like Chaucer, Swift and Jane Austen, who often make their point by deliberately lulling us into a false sense of security or complacency and then deftly twitching the rug from under our feet. Swift, in his famous *Modest Proposal* for simultaneously solving the famine and population problems of Ireland (by having its inhabitants eat their babies) rivets and revolts us by the bland indecency of the suggestion before swinging round upon us with the implied question "Well then, how would **you** solve it?" – which no one has been able to answer then or since.

We may now examine this kind of thing at work in a couple of examples of the ironist's art, from which we may perhaps learn more about the lineaments of verbal irony but which will be chiefly useful in allowing us to feel it in operation. The first comes from Oscar Wilde's critical essay *The Decay of Lying: An Observation,* and takes the form of a dialogue between two young men sitting in the library of a country house in Nottinghamshire:

> *Cyril.* Well, you need not look at the landscape. You can lie on the grass and smoke and talk.
>
> *Vivian.* But Nature is so uncomfortable. Grass is hard and lumpy and damp, and full of dreadful black insects. Why, even Morris' poorest workman could make you a more comfortable seat than the whole of Nature can. Nature pales before the furniture of "the street which from Oxford has borrowed its name," as the poet you love so much once vilely phrased it. I don't complain. If Nature had been comfortable, mankind would never have invented architecture, and I prefer houses to the open air. In a house we all feel of the proper proportions. Everything is subordinated to us, fashioned for our use and our pleasure. Egotism itself, which is so necessary to a proper sense of human dignity, is entirely the result of indoor life. Out of doors one becomes abstract and impersonal. One's individuality absolutely leaves one. And then Nature is so indifferent, so unappreciative. Whenever I am walking in the park here, I always feel that I am no more to her than the cattle that browse on the slope, or the burdock that blooms in the ditch. Nothing is more evident than that Nature hates Mind. Thinking is the most unhealthy thing in the world, and people die of it just as they die of any other disease. Fortunately, in England at any rate, thought is not catching. Our splendid physique as a people is entirely due to our national stupidity. I only hope we shall be able to keep this great historic bulwark of our happiness for many years to come; but I am afraid that we are beginning to be over-educated; at least everybody who is incapable of learning has taken to teaching – that is really what our enthusiasm for education has come to. In the meantime, you had better go back to your wearisome uncomfortable Nature, and leave me to correct my proofs.
>
> *Cyril.* Writing an article! That is not very consistent after what you have just said.
>
> *Vivian.* Who wants to be consistent? The dullard and the doctrinaire, the tedious people who carry out their principles to the bitter end of action, to

the *reductio ad absurdum* of practice. Not I. Like Emerson, I write over the door of my library the word "Whim". Besides, my article is really a most salutary and valuable warning. If it is attended to, there may be a new Renaissance of Art.

Cyril. What is the subject?

Vivian. I intend to call it "The Decay of Lying: A Protest."

Cyril. Lying! I should have thought that our politicians kept up that habit.

Vivian. I assure you that they do not. They never rise beyond the level of misrepresentation, and actually condescend to prove, to discuss, to argue. How different from the temper of the true liar, with his frank, fearless statements, his superb irresponsibility, his healthy, natural disdain of proof of any kind! After all, what is a fine lie? Simply that which is its own evidence. If a man is sufficiently unimaginative to produce evidence in support of a lie, he might just as well speak the truth at once. No, the politicians won't do. Something may, perhaps, be urged on behalf of the Bar. The mantle of the Sophist has fallen on its members. Their feigned ardours and unreal rhetoric are delightful. They can make the worse appear the better cause, as though they were fresh from Leontine schools, and have been known to wrest from reluctant juries triumphant verdicts of acquittal for their clients, even when those clients, as often happens, were clearly and unmistakably innocent. But they are briefed by the prosaic, and are not ashamed to appeal to precedent. In spite of their endeavours, the truth will out. Newspapers, even, have degenerated. They may now be absolutely relied upon. One feels it as one wades through their columns. It is always the unreadable that occurs. I am afraid that there is not much to be said in favour of either the lawyer or the journalist. Besides, what I am pleading for is Lying in art. Shall I read you what I have written? It might do you a good deal of good.[6]

Wilde, working at this early stage of his essay to establish its thesis, touches ironically on a variety of topics: Romantic poetry (the poet quoted is Wordsworth) and its concomitant love of Nature; English national patriotism; the professional aspirations of teachers, politicians, barristers and journalists; the language of Victorian moral approval; even logical consistency itself. Each in its way gets reflected in the distorting mirror of irony, causing us at least to take a fresh look at it and re-examine our own well-worn responses, as we have so often seen irony doing in this chapter. As we thus re-examine these things we will arrive, if the irony works properly, at conclusions that endorse Wilde's own ideas: to question our unthinking enthusiasm for Nature and our habitual unreflecting patriotism reinforces the real importance of what he calls Mind or thought. We must evidently be prepared not only to dismiss our prejudices, but also to keep our wits about us, dangerous though that may prove.

In the second half of the extract Wilde exploits in the same ironic way our prejudices about politicians, lawyers and journalists. As sophisticated citizens we all accept that such people tell lies, though we usually deplore their doing so. The real trouble is, claims Wilde ironically, that they don't lie enough, being restricted by various forms of pragmatism – politicians by debate, lawyers by precedent and accident, journalists by facts, and all of them by what they perceive as the truth. Wilde nevertheless gives them little credit for these concessions: perhaps the crowning moment of the extract comes towards the end of Vivian's final speech with the utterly unexpected but totally 'right' word *innocent* which underlines, among other things, the accidental quality of much justice. The two-facedness thus attributed to all three professions makes Wilde's point: the "true liar" (a phrase worth pondering for its own sake) is *frank* and *fearless*, while "a fine lie" is "that which is its own evidence". Wilde has got us thinking about literature, about (as he finally acknowledges) *Lying in art;* and his irony has pointed this up, and raised questions about the nature of truth, as no other approach could have done. The idea of art's own moral self-sufficiency is not a new one: at the start of Chapter 1 we noted Sir Philip Sidney making very much the same claim in the sixteenth century. Perhaps it is no accident that Wilde sees the reiteration of the idea as likely to trigger off "a new Renaissance in Art".

We may notice one other effect of Wilde's irony here, all the more evident as a result of the particular method he pursues. Perhaps we should not call it Wilde's irony at all, but Vivian's; Wilde in the end must take responsibility for it, but then he is also responsible for the comments of Cyril, who functions somewhat like a comedian's 'straight man'. By shaping his essay (if that's what it is) as a dialogue, Wilde has doubled the thickness of the protective armour with which irony always invest its users. If verbal ironists proceed by meaning something other than what they say, then of course they can, if pressed, readily disclaim either what they say or what they mean: to an outraged lawyer Vivian could conceivably claim that his naive complimentary remarks were to be taken literally, while reassuring the rest of us that his true meaning lay elsewhere. And Wilde could retort furthermore that these are Vivian's opinions anyway, and not necessarily those of his creator – any more than Iago's or Caliban's views represent Shakespeare's. Ironists acquire fall-back positions such as these at the cost, of course, of having their point entirely missed by literalists, as we have seen.

For our other example of irony we will turn to poetry, where we can see it working with most control and precision. In *An Essay on Criticism* the eighteenth century satirist Alexander Pope lists the criteria, each by itself inadequate, by which people judge the merit of a piece of writing. Having dismissed *conceit* ('glittering thoughts struck out in every line') and *language* ('style') he turns to numbers (i.e. versification):

But most by Numbers judge a Poet's song,
And smooth or rough, with them, is right or wrong;
In the bright Muse tho' thousand charms conspire,
Her Voice is all these tuneful fools admire;
Who haunt Parnassus but to please their ear,
Not mend their minds; as some to Church repair,
Not for the doctrine, but the music there.
These equal syllables alone require,
Tho' oft the ear the open vowels tire;
While expletives their feeble aid do join;
And ten low words oft creep in one dull line;
While they ring round the same unvary'd chimes,
With sure returns of still expected rhymes.
Where-e'er you find 'the cooling western breeze,'
In the next line, it 'whispers thro' the trees;'
If crystal streams 'with pleasing murmurs creep,'
The reader's threaten'd (not in vain) with 'sleep.'
Then, at the last and only couplet fraught
With some unmeaning thing they call a thought,
A needless Alexandrine ends the song,
That, like a wounded snake, drags its slow length along.
Leave such to tune their own dull rhymes, and know
What's roundly smooth, or languishingly slow;
And praise the easy vigour of a line
Where Denham's strength, and Waller's sweetness join.
True ease in writing comes from art, not chance,
As those move easiest who have learn'd to dance.
'Tis not enough no harshness gives offence,
The sound must seem an Echo to the sense:
Soft is the strain when Zephyr gently blows,
And the smooth stream in smoother numbers flows;
But when loud surges lash the sounding shoar,
The hoarse, rough verse should like the torrent roar.
When Ajax strives, some rock's vast weight to throw,
The line too labours, and the words move slow;
Not so, when swift Camilla scours the plain,
Flies o'er th'unbending corn, and skims along the main[7]

Pope moves skilfully from parodying bad verse to demonstrating how
poetry should be written, and in the process we learn something about the
important relationship between sound and sense in language – something
that we should perhaps add to our findings about Mimesis in Chapter 1. His
irony operates most obviously and powerfully in the first half of the extract,
where it does nothing less than turn bad verse into good: the faults Pope lists
– *open vowels* (what we today would call 'overuse of the glottal stop'),

pedestrian monosyllables, trite rhymes and so on – become virtues when thus parodied so brilliantly. He exploits the ironic discrepancy between the superficial effect such poetry has on its 'tunefully foolish' alazons and the delight it affords those of us who perceive this instance of it to be parody. Both effects, simultaneously sustained, culminate in a kind of grammatical pun on *sleep*, where we enjoy the tension between 'sleep' the *word* and 'sleep' the *thing*.

But the second half of the extract also contains irony. Perhaps of a less obvious kind, this nevertheless comes close to some of the linguistic issues we have already discussed in this book. Pope purports to be demonstrating ways in which language can most effectively imitate certain phenomena – the West Wind, a storm, Ajax and Camilla at their activities; but merely to point this out reminds us at once that we are really dealing with *poesis* rather than with *mimesis*. Pope has conjured these phenomena out of nowhere, and his verse is in fact creating its own reality rather than merely imitating something already in existence – and doing this so well that we hardly realise what's happening. He tactfully points this out to us in the often misquoted metaphor

> The sound must seem an Echo to the sense

– *seem*, not *be*, because the sense is not there at all until the sound conspires with other aspects of the language to create it. Perhaps in the end it is the perpetual tension we perceive between its poetic and mimetic functions that endows language with its essential ambiguity and generates inexhaustibly fascinating irony for those writers and readers sensitive enough to feel it.

Notes

1 see Chapter 2, and Johnson pp. 677ff.
2 Byron *Don Juan* I, CCII-CCIII
3 Corneille Vol. I, p.343
4 Pound pp. 64-5
5 Matthew 7:1-2
6 Wilde pp. 291-2
7 Pope, Alexander *An Essay on Criticism* 337-372

6

SUBJECTIVITY AND POINT OF VIEW

(Alice didn't venture to ask what he paid
them with; and so you see I can't tell you)
Lewis Carroll

In our discussion of Mimesis in Chapter 1 we noticed, with some scepticism, the way certain writers try to impart an aura of **objectivity** to their writing by using the passive voice. No evidence seems to have turned up since then to dissuade us from this scepticism; indeed, our examination of ideas about *correctness* in particular should have confirmed our doubts. We must now, therefore, face up to the **subjectivity** which indwells all language, spoken and written, clarify the term as far as possible, and suggest how we may put our awareness of it to use as readers and writers.

If we use the word *subjective* at all, most of us probably do so in one – or a mixture – of four senses. The first, and commonest, treats the word somewhat pejoratively, as a regrettable, even culpable, alternative to the objective detachment with which we would like to view things. If I say "I am taking a subjective view" my hearer will almost certainly detect a hint of apology in my words, and will understand me to be confessing that some personal consideration or some deficiency peculiar to myself makes me an inadequate witness on the subject in hand. If I were more magnanimous, or more intelligent, or if I could somehow permanently reach the state of detachment which my confession itself hints at, then I might be better worth listening to. As it is . . .

From this sense we may distinguish another one, very much more morally neutral. *Subjective* may in certain circumstances mean much the same as *individual* and identify those qualities which make each of us a unique human being, a self not quite like any other self on the surface of or in the history of this world. This sense, which has no doubt grown stronger with the rise of democracy and the growing importance of the individual – as well as with psychological and sociological studies which refer to the person under observation as *the subject* – passes less judgement on any resultant behaviour; indeed, it may abolish all distinction between good and bad, right and wrong, validating claims such as "I know what I like" or endorsing statements like Dr Johnson's "sensation is sensation" (i.e. we feel what we feel and that's all there is to it). Alone and unqualified, this version of the word probably leans towards that state of individual isolation philosophers know as *solipsism,* which *The Oxford Dictionary* defines as 'The view or theory that self is the only object of real knowledge or the only thing really existent.'

Quite close to this sits another sense, equally neutral, which identifies attitudes or experiences which particular groups of individuals have in common as a result of some shared background – whether biological, ethnic or cultural. Thus we can distinguish feminine from masculine subjectivity, oriental from western, Maori from Pakeha, adult from juvenile and so on. The idea assumes that, from the start, our backgrounds have subjected us to a good deal of conditioning much – even most – of which we can and should do very little to counter. Indeed, without it we lose identity, and it generates much of the value of what we as individuals bring to society as a whole. It resists any claim to superiority by any one group or culture, just as we saw modern linguistic scholarship, in Chapter 4, resisting the 'correctness' of the South-east Midland dialect of English. Perhaps the most important cultural phenomenon of the second half of the twentieth century has been the explosive literary expression of feminine subjectivity – no less than half the human race thus finding a voice and discovering an identity, to the incalculable benefit of the race as a whole (and certainly to the edification of all *man*kind). Minority groups are expressing their own subjectivity with growing freedom and confidence too; and where literature leads, popular opinion and political change eventually follow.

One other sense of the word may be worth considering – a sense founded on *subject* meaning 'knower' (the person who experiences, the cognitive self) and on *object* meaning 'the thing apprehended' (the reality 'out there'). *Subjectivity* in this sense must recognize, however, that this *object* also includes the perceiving self, and that cognition in some ways comes round upon itself. Literature – indeed all writing, whether 'literary' or not – constantly wrestles with the paradox implicit in this; hence our concern as writers with ideas of *persona,* authorial presence, and point of view. The statement "I am taking a subjective view" may serve as an example. In it, *I* (as subject) make a statement about myself (as object). I thus split myself into two – a fallible subjective self, and an infallible (?objective) self who is passing this judgement on the fallible one. The assumption that *I* expect you to believe the statement may even identify a third self lurking behind the other two. All this may sound more like metaphysics than 'writing', but it is useful in reminding us of the complexities that underlie any use of the first-person pronoun and the whole question of **point of view** in general.

For if we can never achieve objectivity in our use of language, we must learn to identify and acknowledge whichever of the above kinds of subjectivity attaches to our writing, and not only live with it but turn it to our advantage. In other words, since we will inevitably be bringing a certain point of view to whatever we write we will do well to learn ways of handling it tactfully, honestly and effectively. Most of us will already have learnt that anyone writing a narrative of any kind faces a plain, though fundamental, choice, before beginning to write, between first and third-person points of view.

If we choose a *first-person narrator* we must be prepared, on the face of it at any rate, to swamp our own personalities entirely: Mark Twain so chooses in *Huckleberry Finn,* where the reader enjoys the advantages of listening to Huck at some length and finding out a great deal about him – not all he knows, perhaps, since he may well hold some things back; but we may often compensate by guessing things that Huck is not even aware of himself. That indeed is one of the main pleasures of the book, since Twain habitually exploits the ambiguity we have just seen attaching to the word 'I' and the ironic effects it generates. But in other ways a first-person narrative limits writers, particularly in the amount of information they can convey to their audience; however much they hint at or imply, they must remain within their narrator's horizon and ignore events that occur beyond it.

This problem disappears if we opt to write our story from an *omniscient third-person* point of view. Here we can say what we like, since we know everything. That, however, is a very dangerous level of knowledge, since it presumably includes how things are going to turn out in the end, and we will be hard put to justify keeping our reader in suspense. It also conflicts with the story-teller's bounden duty to select and limit the material of the story: no one wants, or has time, to be told everything. Thus Lewis Carroll follows Alice through Wonderland and the Looking-Glass country, telling us – for some of the time at least – what he wants us to know when he wants us to know it:

> The Queen gasped, and sat down: the rapid journey through the air had quite taken away her breath, and for a minute or two she could do nothing but hug

the little Lily in silence. As soon as she had recovered her breath a little, she called out to the White King, who was sitting sulkily among the ashes, "Mind the volcano!"

"What volcano?" said the King, looking up anxiously into the fire, as if he thought that was the most likely place to find one.[1]

But Carroll either cannot or chooses not to sustain this sort of thing for more than a few lines. Subjectivity of some sort or other commonly intervenes very quickly. We can see the beginning of it even in this short passage: the phrase "as soon as she had recovered her breath a little" takes us partway into the experience of the White Queen, while the King's response ("anxiously . . . as if he thought . . .") firmly and unequivocally identifies and endorses his point of view.

  Carroll quickly and willingly slips, that is to say, into a *limited third-person* narrative, the technique whereby he focuses on one of the participants in his story – most commonly Alice herself – and confines himself within her knowledge and experience of the events of the story. This method too holds enormous potential for irony, since the reader is often likely to be unsure whether the words represent Carroll's view of things or Alice's.

It would be nice to complete a tidy picture at this point by discussing the merits and demerits of *second-person* narrative technique. This, unfortunately, is very rare, and impossible to sustain: *Winnie-the-Pooh* flirts with it to begin with:

When he put it like this, you saw how it was, and you aimed very carefully at the balloon, and fired.

"*Ow!*" said Pooh.

"Did I miss?" you asked.

"You didn't exactly *miss*," said Pooh, "but you missed the *balloon*".

"I'm so sorry," you said, and you fired again, and this time you hit the balloon, and the air came slowly out, and Winnie-the-Pooh floated down to the ground.[2]

Second and third-person narratives alternate in this extract. Immediately after it the book reverts, and sticks, entirely to the third person.

Choice of narrative point of view perhaps emerges from all this as less 'plain' than I suggested a moment ago. It certainly remains fundamental. We find Virginia Woolf facing up to some possible complexities when discussing with herself, in her diary for 1929, some of her problems as a writer:

Yesterday morning I made another start on *The Moths,* but that won't be its title; and several problems cry out at once to be solved. Who thinks it? And am I outside the thinker? One wants some device which is not a trick.[3]

Some eighteen months later, the same preoccupation surfaces as she celebrates, in understandably incoherent prose, the end of the first draft of the same book:

> Here in the few minutes that remain, I must record, heaven be praised, the end of *The Waves*. I wrote the words O Death fifteen minutes ago, having reeled across the last ten pages with some moments of such intensity and intoxication that I seemed only to stumble after my own voice, or almost, after some sort of speaker (as when I was mad) I was almost afraid, remembering the voices that used to fly ahead. Anyhow, it is done; and I have been sitting these 15 minutes in a state of glory, and calm, and some tears . . .[4]

It sounds as though Woolf's early question "Am I outside the speaker?" was never to get a clear answer – nor, in the light of what we have seen so far about subjectivity, would we expect it to. Who, in the end, am *I*? And will language ever serve fully to isolate and identify me?

Since total objectivity clearly remains beyond our reach we must answer No to that last question. How can I be sure what I'm talking about if I'm not even sure who I am? How can I trust the picture if I don't even trust the camera? The human mind by no means enjoys this kind of insecurity, and people try various ways of by-passing or even short-circuiting it. We have already noticed how the passive voice of the verb offers some illusions of certainty. It does this by withholding information: a committee meeting minute to the effect that "It was decided that a letter should be sent . . ." conceals both those who took the decision and those responsible for sending the letter (and will mean, in the absence of an exceptionally conscientious secretary or chairperson, that it will probably never even get written).

But what the eye doesn't see, the heart doesn't normally agonize over, so that most writers of documents such as research reports still favour phrases like "A sample was taken" or "A change of colour was observed", redolent though these are of the mechanical or clockwork universe postulated by nineteenth century scientists who clearly thought that the observer made not the slightest difference to the thing observed and that you could make objective statements about anything if you tried hard enough. It is hard to assess the damage such an attitude has done to the world we live in, especially by 'observers' like anthropologists and others who make it their business to study human beings.

When we read any piece of writing, uncertainties caused by its inevitable subjectivity may well tempt us to search for 'the truth' by studying the person who wrote it – the woman or man behind the words. This too bears little fruit in the end, for one or more of at least three reasons: if we succeed in identifying the author's intentions, we do so in words, and our problem therefore remains; we have no guarantee that the author's intentions survive in the printed page; and, as we saw in Chapter 3, the author's intentions, assuming we could ascertain them, only partly account for the meaning of the passage at the best of times. We do well to heed T. S. Eliot who, to the enquiry "Mr Eliot, what did you mean by the line 'Lady, three white leopards sat under a juniper-tree'?" is said to have replied, "I think I meant 'Lady, three white leopards sat under a juniper-tree'."[5]

Nor is there any use bypassing authors' intentions in the search for some ulterior truth about them, psychological or otherwise. Again, we have to use words, and in them no objectivity lies. And such biographical evidence as we have assures us of the futility of trying to link writers' or artists' life experiences too closely with the works they produced: Mozart's music betrays little of the stresses of his life, and we try to reconstruct Shakespeare's biography from his writings at our peril. As Northrop Frye reminds us:

> Shakespeare, as a personality, was so self-effacing that he has irritated some people into a frenzy of trying to prove that he never existed.[6]

In any case, we are approaching the logical absurdity of using writers' works in order to reconstruct their lives and opinions in order to explain their works. We do better to stick with what we've got – the finished, published product (or as near to it as the labours of bibliographers and editors can get us) – and learn to live with its ineluctable subjectivity. We should not, by now, be surprised to find truth of another kind replacing and compensating for the Gradgrindian 'facts' that so perseveringly elude us.[7]

We may test this in some examples. The first, an extract from Russian poet Irina Ratushinskaya's book *Grey is the Colour of Hope*, describes a moment of crisis during her years as a political prisoner. Ratushinskaya wrote in Russian; an English translation, no matter how good, inevitably compounds problems of subjectivity. Whatever the detailed verbal effects of the original, we must content ourselves with responding to those in front of us.

> As for me, I sit down to work. On the table, I lay out all my letters from home, as well as an unfinished one of my own. However, correspondence is

not what I'm about. In minute letters, I write out my latest poems on four centimetre wide strips of cigarette paper. This is one of our ways of getting information out of the Zone. These strips of cigarette paper are then tightly rolled into a small tube (less than the thickness of your little finger), sealed and made moisture-proof by a method of our own devising, and handed on when a suitable opportunity presents itself. I mention this procedure because it is one already known to the KGB. One such 'capsule' was intercepted and Novikov, one of the camp officers, showed it to me in triumph, hinting at the possibility of an additional sentence. But in the summer of 1983 this method was still unknown to the KGB.

I become so engrossed in my work that I do not hear the stamp of boots, nor do I get a chance to conceal my handiwork before duty officer Kiselyova looms in the doorway. Desperately, I seize the only chance I have and slide the tiny strips with my poems under the jumble of letters on the table. Kiselyova (devil take her for arriving at such an inopportune moment!) hovers beside me: "Writing a letter, are you?"

Without warning, she grabs my unfinished letter, exposing my poor defencelesss strips of poetry for all to see. The only hope I have is to focus her full attention on the letter.

"Give it back this minute! You're not the censor to read my mail!"

Thank God she takes the bait, and jerks away her hand without releasing the letter.

"Maybe this is not a letter at all? I've got to check."

"You can see for yourself that the opening words are 'Greetings to you all, my loved ones', so it's clearly a letter."

"Not necessarily," maintains Kiselyova, while all the time the wheels are going round in that thick head of hers: it's true that she has no right to act as a censor, yet how can she tell whether this is a letter or not without reading it? Some problem I've set her.

At this moment Tatyana Mikhailovna comes into the room and, sizing up the situation in a flash, enters the debate: "Never mind prying into other people's letters. You should be ashamed of yourself. Don't you have enough family matters of your own to think about without poking your nose into other people's?"

"I don't care about her family affairs," blusters Kiselyova, but she is on the retreat. "It's my job to check whether this is a letter or something else."

"There are plenty of officers to do that. You can tell from the opening words that it's a letter, and that's enough. No reason for you to take on other people's responsibilities!"

Kiselyova is obviously not keen to get involved in a row. She did not come into the room with any specific aim in mind and, though she is loth to admit it, only seized on my letter out of curiosity to see what these 'politicals' write to their husbands. She thrusts back the letter and waddles away.

Oh, the tongue-lashing I got from Tatyana Mikhailovna! Never mind that all ended well – but my carelessness! I'd come within a breath of being caught, of giving away our method to the KGB. That would have led to searches, intensification of surveillance, and then what would our chances be of getting any information out of the camp? Couldn't I have asked somebody to stand watch? There was nothing I could say to justify myself, so I stood there meekly under the thunderbolts of her strictures. Of course, the 'post mortem' was conducted outside, away from the concealed microphones in the house. Finally, Tatyana Mikhailovna relented: after all, I had not lost my head and did manage to deflect Kiselyova's attention elsewhere. But the reprimands Tatyana Mikhailovna rained down on my head that day were to serve me in good stead, for they put an end to any remnants I had of pre-arrest lackadaisical trust in chance. Never again were our secret labours placed under threat of exposure by the KGB through carelessness on my part: I was never caught. Yet there were plenty of people besides me to be caught in our complex information network, so we had both successes and failures. However, by one means or another, everything became known 'outside' sooner or later. Understandably, this infuriated the KGB, but they were forced to admit that they were powerless to stop us.[8]

We may first notice the immediacy of this narrative style. Ratushinskaya writes in the first person: these are, after all, things that have happened to her. She also chooses to use the present tense, thus telling a calculated 'lie': these things are not in fact happening to her now, nor even while she is writing about them (as we might naively suppose the present tense to indicate). Her use of the present tense drags the past into the present (or vice versa), allowing her to recreate far more truthfully – and us to experience far more vividly – the tensions of the experience. We accept that the event itself has mercifully passed into history (although 1983 remains horrifyingly recent). Ratushinskaya's verbal re-creation of it gains immediacy and compulsion partly from the dialogue and partly because of the way the present tense modifies the first-person viewpoint: it pushes into the background one manifestation of the narrative *I* that might otherwise have got in the way: it focuses all our attention on the *I* as we meet it in the narrative, writing, fearing, desperately manoeuvring, and finally quailing under Mikhailovna's "thunderbolts"; but this makes us largely forget the *I* of the later Ratushinskaya, after her release and migration to the West, sitting down at her writing-table in 1987 or whenever it was – the *I* of now as opposed to the *I* of then. Both *personae* remain, of course; but the earlier, suffering one catches almost all the limelight.

Thus Ratushinskaya rivets our attention to her immediate point of view; the translation probably differs little from the original in the way it achieves this. We can be less certain, however, about some of the more detailed effects of the passage and of the point of view it adopts. On at least three occasions this shifts so that we see things from some perspective different from, or additional to – it is very hard to tell – that of the narrator.

Kiselyova's "thick head" seems to be pure Ratushinskaya: like "waddles away" later on, its connotations, in English at least, are pejorative enough to render any other possibility unlikely; likewise the notion of "wheels going round" in it. Nevertheless we also gain momentary glimpses of what those *wheels* are producing in Kiselyova's consciousness – first, perplexity about "how she can tell whether this is a letter or not without reading it", and a little later "curiosity to see what these 'politicals' write to their husbands". If we doubt these shifts of viewpoint, the phrase "these politicals", which, apart from the quotation marks, seems pure Kiselyova, should reassure us of their existence.

So far, the narrator's handling of point of view has inclined us strongly in her favour. She is in present danger, which we share; she is thinking quickly, and we approve; and she is outwitting (literally, by externalizing her ideas) the rebarbative Kiselyova, which we enjoy. The effect is all the more salutary, therefore, when the narrative makes its other major shift in point of view and we suddenly see things through Tatyana Mikhailovna's eyes – indeed catch (probably) the very tone and cadence of her voice in phrases like "but my carelessness!" and questions like "Couldn't I have asked somebody to stand watch?" The narrator withholds nothing of her disgrace. We nevertheless remain firmly in sympathy with her, perhaps because these strictures come clearly filtered through her point of view (*my, I*). This not only enhances our sense of her humility, but also underlines the strength of her self-awareness. What is more, it contributes a powerfully ironic tone to this stage of the story. An able writer, far from attempting to circumvent her subjectivity in her efforts to tell the truth, has triumphantly acknowledged and celebrated it, gaining our full assent in the process. "One wants some device which is not a trick" wrote Virginia Woolf in her diary; Ratushinskaya seems to have found that device. Perhaps it is a trick; if so, it's one played in the open, and played with integrity, truth and love.

And it so closely resembles the kinds of device used by writers of first-person narrative fiction that we may well question the distinction we commonly draw between 'creative' and 'non-creative' writing. *Historicity*, to which we normally and instinctively attribute the 'truth' of genres like biography and autobiography, becomes – on closer inspection and in the absence of time-machines – an elusive and unreliable criterion. In practice, as the Ratushinskaya extract demonstrates, we judge according to some other principle, some quality of integrity which both 'creative' and 'non-creative' writing share in common, some *mimetic* or *poetic* truth of language. Whatever it is, it comes very close to the heart of our humanity, and may prove, in the end, to be the most precious thing we possess.

A writer of narrative – whether of fiction, like Lewis Carroll, or of autobiography, like Irina Ratushinskaya – must acknowledge and exploit point of view. This assertion clearly holds true of any kind of narrative writing, and we could illustrate it from any of the other writers quoted so far in this book. We may test its relevance to writing of a more *expository* kind – essays, reports and so on – by examining the beginning of the nineteenth century English writer William Hazlitt's essay *On Familiar Style,* in which he argues for reverting from the inflated, circuitous sub-Johnsonian writing of the previous century to something more nearly allied to ordinary speech:

It is not easy to write a familiar style. Many people mistake a familiar for a vulgar style, and suppose that to write without affectation is to write at random. On the contrary, there is nothing that requires more precision, and, if I may so say, purity of expression, than the style I am speaking of. It utterly rejects not only all unmeaning pomp, but all low, cant phrases, and loose, unconnected, *slipshod* allusions. It is not to take the first word that offers, but the best word in common use; it is not to throw words together in any combinations we please, but to follow and avail ourselves of the true idiom of the language. To write a genuine familiar or truly English style, is to write as any one would speak in common conversation, who had a thorough command and choice of words, or who could discourse with ease, force, and perspicuity, setting aside all pedantic and oratorical flourishes. Or to give another illustration, to write naturally is the same thing in regard to common conversation, as to read naturally is in regard to common speech. It does not follow that it is an easy thing to give the true accent and inflection of the words you utter, because you do not attempt to rise above the level of ordinary life and colloquial speaking. You do not assume indeed the solemnity of the pulpit, or the tone of stage-declamation: neither are you at liberty to gabble on at a venture, without emphasis or discretion, or to resort to vulgar dialect or clownish pronunciation. You must steer a middle course. You are tied down to a given and appropriate articulation, which is determined by the habitual associations between sense and sound, and which you can only hit by entering into the author's meaning, as you must find the proper words and style to express yourself by fixing your thoughts on the subject you have to write about. Any one may mouth out a passage with a theatrical cadence, or get upon stilts to tell his thoughts: but to write or speak with propriety or simplicity is a more difficult task. Thus it is easy to affect a pompous style, to use a word twice as big as the thing you want to express: it is not so easy to pitch upon the very word that exactly fits it. Out of eight or ten words equally common, equally intelligible, with nearly equal pretensions, it is a matter of some nicety and discrimination to pick out the very one, the preferableness of which is scarcely perceptible, but decisive.[9]

Each generation has to disencumber itself of cliché and find its own voice in this way, and Hazlitt's remarks make an interesting comparison with those of George Orwell in *Politics and the English Language* over a century later.[10] Meanwhile he makes, and sustains, his point by his persuasive handling of his own subjectivity.

Quite early in the piece Hazlitt acknowledges that these are indeed his own opinions by introducing the first-person pronoun *I*. At the same time he creates the pretence, by no means uncommon among writers and particularly appropriate here, that he is *speaking* rather than writing to us. Thus a formal essay, whose constituent parts the writer has clearly shaped and balanced with considerable care, acquires some of the relaxation of an easy chat. A few lines later Hazlitt can consequently introduce with equal effectiveness the informal *you,* so avoiding the ponderous repetition of third-person devices like *one* or *the writer* (which today, of course, would in its turn generate further problems like the sexist *he,* the clumsy *he or she* or the unmanageable *(s)he*).

By doing all these things he openly shoulders responsibility for the connotations of his words and phrases: *vulgar* (meaning *low-class* rather than *obscene*), *purity, genuine, gabble, mouth out, discrimination* and so on, together with the metaphors he invents (*throw, tied down, hit, get upon stilts, pitch upon*) all embody his subjectivity and reflect in their various ways the strong emotional bias he brings to his topic. But at no stage do we feel that he is in any way tricking or browbeating us into agreeing with him, in the way that advertising copy so often does (counterproductively, if we have our wits about us). Hazlitt has a case to make, and he makes it the more effectively by coming into the open to do so. His writing thus works as active testimony in support of 'the familiar style' he is championing, and may – like that of Irina Ratushinskaya and any good writer – remind us that writing calls upon its practitioners to make an endless series of moral as well as verbal choices, and tests our integrity as much as our vocabulary.

Notes

1 Carroll p. 137
2 Milne pp. 17-18
3 Woolf p. 146
4 Woolf p. 169
5 The line begins Part II of *Ash-Wednesday*
6 Frye p. 16
7 see Chapter 3
8 Ratushinskaya pp. 66-8
9 Hazlitt Vol. 8, pp. 242-3
10 see Chapter 1, p. 4

7

THE WRITING PROCESS

> Always speak the truth – think before you speak – and
> write it down afterwards.
>
> *The Red Queen*

In this chapter we examine the writing process by subdividing it into six
separate stages. To do so necessarily oversimplifies what is in reality a very
complex and many-layered business indeed, but some such artificial division
is helpful in allowing us to investigate the many facets of the reality – and
we have long since established, in any case, that language approaches 'the
truth' only by way of a variety of distortions (exploiting 'lies' like metaphor,
irony and indeed words themselves). The six stages – **invention,
discussion, drafting, revision, proof-reading** and **publication** certainly
exist: but to name them like this suggests, quite erroneously, that they exist
separately and even that they occur in the order given. All in fact co-exist
simultaneously – and together produce an experience quite unlike any one
of them in isolation. Words, as usual, are not big enough to name and trace
the whole experience, so, as usual, we must abstract and simplify in order to
say anything at all. We may even learn something by articulating the
experience into words. That, again, is usual.

Where does a piece of writing start? Who would be bold enough to
codify the processes and mysteries of **invention**? They seem to range
widely, varying at the very least from the voice of the Holy Spirit at one end
of the scale to an editorial deadline near the other. But are even those two
so very different, or always separable? Good, and occasionally great,
journalism emerges under the pressure of the latter; Shakespeare had to
finish his plays in time for scheduled performance; and St Paul, having
dictated his *Epistle to the Colossians,* no doubt scribbled its postscript while
Tychicus, his messenger, stood by to bear it off. And flowers bloom in the
most unlikely corners: even birthday and Christmas cards, those perennial

cornucopias of doggerel, have generated at least one poetic masterpiece, T.S. Eliot's *Journey of the Magi*.

Writers in general have been ready enough to describe their more exciting moments of invention. These may coincide with, and perhaps result from, one of life's major crises:

> In 1937, during the war in Spain, when I found myself in prison with the prospect of facing a firing squad, I made a vow: if ever I got out of there alive I would write an autobiography so frank and unsparing of myself that it would make Rousseau's *Confessions* and the *Memoirs* of Cellini appear as sheer cant.[1]

Or they may emerge in the course of daily routine:

> I have this moment, while having a bath, conceived an entire new book – a sequel to *A Room of One's Own* – about the sexual life of women: to be called Professions of Women perhaps – Lord how exciting![2]

They may result from sheer boredom and irritation:

> More discontents I never had
> Since I was born, than here,
> Where I have been and still am sad,
> In this dull Devonshire,
> Yet justly too I must confess
> I ne'er invented such
> Ennobled numbers for the press
> Than where I loathed so much.[3]

Or they may arise as the last desperate skirmish in the battle against starvation:

> 'I must do something,' said I, as I sat that night in my lonely apartment, with some bread and a pitcher of water before me.
> Thereupon taking some of the bread, and eating it, I considered what I was to do. 'I have no idea what I am to do,' said I, as I stretched my hand towards the pitcher, 'unless – and here I took a considerable draught – I write a tale or a novel –. That bookseller,' I continued, speaking to myself, 'is certainly much in need of a tale or novel, otherwise he would not advertise for one. Suppose I write one, I appear to have no other chance of extricating myself from my present difficulties; surely it was Fate that conducted me to his window.'
> 'I will do it,' said I, as I struck my hand against the table; 'I will do it.'

Suddenly a heavy cloud of despondency came over me. Could I do it? Had I the imagination requisite to write a tale or a novel? 'Yes, yes,' said I, as I struck my hand again against the table, ' I can manage it; give me fair play, and I can accomplish anything.'

But should I have fair play? I must have something to maintain myself with whilst I wrote my tale, and I had but eighteen pence in the world. Would that maintain me whilst I wrote my tale? Yes, I thought it would, provided I ate bread, which did not cost much, and drank water, which cost nothing: it was a poor diet, it was true, but better men than myself had written on bread and water . . .

It was true there was my lodging to pay for; but up to the present time I owed nothing, and perhaps, by the time that the people of the house asked me for money, I should have written a tale or a novel, which would bring me in money; I had paper, pens, and ink, and let me not forget them, I had candles in my closet, all paid for, to light me during my night-work. Enough, I would go doggedly to work upon my tale or novel.

But what was the tale or novel to be about? . . . I want a character for my hero, thought I . . . why should I not write the adventures of Colonel B — of Londonderry, in Ireland?

Of his life I had inserted an account in the 'Newgate Lives and Trials'; it was bare and meagre, and written in the stiff, awkward style of the seventeenth century; it had, however, strongly captivated my imagination, and I now thought that out of it something better could be made; that, if I added to the adventures and purified the style, I might fashion out of it a very decent tale or novel. On a sudden, however, the proverb of mending old garments with new cloth occurred to me. 'I am afraid,' said I, 'any new adventures which I can invent will not fadge well with the old tale; one will but spoil the other.' I had better have nothing to do with Colonel B ---, thought I, but boldly and independently sit down and write the life of Joseph Sell.

This Joseph Sell, dear reader, was a fictitious personage who had just come into my head. I had never heard of the name, but just at that moment it happened to come into my head; I would write an entirely fictitious narrative, called the 'Life and Adventures of Joseph Sell, the Great Traveller.'

I had better begin at once . . .[4]

These accounts, however much detail they give us of attendant circumstances, still of course tell us little or nothing about where the ideas themselves really come from. That remains a mystery, which we can never approach except by means of terms like *inspiration* (a metaphor from breathing), *Muse* (a personification from classical mythology), *imagination* (the Latin word for picture-making) and some other terms which we will notice at the very end this chapter. All of which may suggest to us why instruction in 'creative writing' possesses only limited value and ought to remain very much on the margins of academic activity.

> . . . the university does not try to foster the social conditions under which great literature can be produced. In the first place, we do not know what these conditions are; in the second place, we have no reason to suppose that they are good conditions. Just as doctors are busiest in an epidemic, so our dramatists and novelists may find their best subjects where decadence, brutality, or idiocy show human behaviour in its more fundamental patterns. Or the producer of literature himself may be a drunk, a homosexual, a Fascist, a philanderer; in short, he may want things that the university cannot guarantee to supply.[5]

Even the more humdrum 'non-creative' forms of writing, where the writer has to meet some obligation imposed from outside – a student fulfilling an assigned essay task, perhaps, a journalist covering a news-story, or a scientist writing a research report – demand invention, though usually of a less spectacular sort than those we have just observed. Student, journalist and scientist all depend on a thesis or 'angle' to focus and illuminate their topic. Such things also wait upon invention.

We all, that is to say, need to discover ways of invoking our own Muses or of opening up the lungs of our imagination to inspiration. Indeed, the overtones of physical exercise present in that last phrase are well worth attending to: the poet Wordsworth " always wrote (if he could) walking up and down a straight gravel-walk, or in some spot where the continuity of his verse met with no collateral interruption". His friend Coleridge, on the other hand, "liked to compose in walking over uneven ground, or breaking through the straggling branches of a copse-wood."[6] Readers of their poetry will understand their preferences. Much even of this book that you are reading now has taken shape during the brisk twenty-five minute walks that, weather permitting, take me to work and back each day. Writing can obviously occur well out of reach of pen or keyboard, when ideas, like Wordsworth's daffodils

> flash upon that inward eye
> Which is the bliss of solitude.

Wordsworth, defining poetry as "the spontaneous overflow of powerful feelings," acknowledged, as we have already seen, that it resulted from "emotion recollected in tranquillity", when presumably the writer has the leisure and detachment to find the most fitting words to recreate the experience. We need to distance ourselves from a subject – or object – to see it more clearly: the best war poetry is rarely written in the trenches (though Ralph Vaughan Williams may well compose his *Pastoral Symphony* there).

But we must not legislate, even for healthy living. Invention may come when we are stale, or sick. We may need coffee (like Stephen Spender), tea (like W.H Auden), tobacco (like Walter de la Mare), or the smell of rotten apples (like the eighteenth century German poet Schiller). Hart Crane after meditating a poem for months or even years, would eventually "charm [it] out of its hiding-place by drinking and laughing and playing the phonograph".[7] Rudyard Kipling demanded the blackest of black ink, and only certain types of pen; "with a lead pencil I ceased to express – probably because I had to use a pencil in reporting".[8]

Perhaps we may tentatively conclude from these confidences that except in special cases like journalism this 'first' stage of writing demands time. An idea may manifest itself suddenly, even in a way that seems somehow outside time. But it has probably been quietly developing, in some remote recesses of the 'subconscious' mind long before that, and may equally need further gestation time before emerging into the light of the day:

> The fine delight that fathers thought; the strong
> Spur, live and lancing like the blowpipe flame,
> Breathes once and, quenchèd faster than it came,
> Leaves yet the mind the mother of immortal song.
> Nine months she then, nay years, nine years she long
> Within her wears, bears, cares and combs the same:
> The widow of an insight lost she lives, with aim
> Now known and hand at work now never wrong.
>   Sweet fire the sire of muse, my soul needs this;
> I want the one rapture of an inspiration.
> O then if in my lagging lines you miss
> The roll, the rise, the carol, the creation,
> My winter world, that scarcely breathes that bliss
> Now, yields you, with some sighs, our explanation.[9]

The *nine months, nine years* or whatever other interval ensues between the orgasmic moment of invention and the pangs of verbal parturition provide opportunity for the next stage, **discussion** – though we must again remind ourselves that this represents an over-simplification, since discussion may also contribute to invention and modify or even abolish the original idea as time passes.

In so far as it has separate existence, however, this rather more mundane stage of the writing process serves two purposes: it articulates into words whatever our invention has suggested, and by its name reminds us that, as we saw William Hazlitt suggesting in Chapter 6, our written language ought never to stray too far from the immediacy and vigour of speech. Professional writers form writers' circles expressly to try out their work on each other before going public; academics take sabbatical leave in order to talk to their colleagues round the world for similar purposes; Lewis Carroll told his immortal stories to the Liddell children and their friends before writing up his creations as *Alice in Wonderland* and *Through the Looking-Glass and what Alice found there;* and most of us derive great benefit from a listening ear into which we can pour our ideas before writing them down. Rephrasing an idea, aloud, often clarifies it and facilitates writing. Teachers of writing all know that a student struggling to express an idea can usually be helped by some such question as "What are you really trying to say?" Modern 'peer-editing' techniques for teaching writing provide systematic opportunity for answering this question, helping, as gently as possible, to excavate ideas from students' private and delicate inner worlds and to toughen them in preparation for exposure to the light of publication.

In the absence of the listening ear, most of us can readily internalize the discussion, switching roles from that of author to that of audience and back again, testing phrases on our tongues and monitoring the ways in which our ideas are developing as we articulate them into words. Like invention, discussion of this sort goes on throughout the writing process; we never stop listening to ourselves – and even after publication continue to hear, with some embarrassment, things that, in retrospect, we would probably rather not have said.

Writers seem, not surprisingly, to have been less interested in describing this more routine stage of the writing process: when you have discussed your ideas you want to get on with drafting them rather than with recording the discussion itself. James Boswell, fortunately, proves an exception. His *Life of Johnson,* founded upon his devouring interest in everything to do with the great man, retails snippets of the kind of conversation wise lexicographers must indulge in:

> On Monday, March 23, I found him busy, preparing a fourth edition of his folio Dictionary. Mr Peyton, one of his original amanuenses, was writing for him. I put him in mind of a meaning of the word *side,* which he had omitted, viz. relationship; as father's side, mother's side. He inserted it. I asked him if *humiliating* was a good word. He said, he had seen it frequently used, but he did not know it to be legitimate English. He would not admit *civilisation* but only *civility.* With great deference to him, I thought *civilisation,* from *to civilise* better in the sense opposed to *barbarity* than *civility;* it is better to have a distinct

word for each sense, than one word with two senses, which *civility* is, in his way of using it.[10]

Under this brief exchange lie all the tensions between authority and experience, between tradition and innovation, and between prescription and description that we saw in our study of correctness in Chapter 4. In addition to this, Boswell conveys some of the personal conflicts that such discussion inevitably provokes: writers are properly jealous of their ideas, even if opposed "with great deference". And perhaps having given way on one point stiffens Johnson's resistance to the others, regardless of their merits.

We need not be surprised, therefore, that some writers remain wary of the stresses of discussion, particularly in the later stages of composition. Edward Gibbon, chronicling his production of *The Decline and Fall of the Roman Empire,* describes himself as having become

> . . . soon disgusted with the modest practice of reading the manuscript to my friends. Of such friends some will praise from politeness, and some will criticize from vanity. The author himself is the best judge of his own performance; none has so deeply meditated on the subject; none is so sincerely interested in the event.[11]

Gibbon nevertheless persevered in lengthy preliminary discussion of another kind: as a scholar, writing history, he found it necessary to pursue a great deal of *research,* which he clearly views as itself an exchange of ideas:

> In a free conversation with books and men, it would be endless to enumerate the names and characters of all who are introduced to our acquaintance; but in this general acquaintance we may select the degrees of friendship and esteem. According to the wise maxim, *Multum legere potius quam multa* [to read intensively rather than widely], I reviewed, again and again, the immortal works of the French and English, the Latin and Italian classics. My Greek studies (though less assiduous than I designed) maintained and extended my knowledge of that incomparable idiom. Homer and Xenophon were still my favourite authors; and I had almost prepared for the press an *Essay on the Cyropaedia* which, in my own judgement, is not unhappily laboured.[12]

Whatever kind of discussion we engage in, the moment eventually arrives when we must get something down for ourselves on parchment, on paper or on the screen of the word-processor (even if, like St Paul and Dr Johnson, we engage someone to take dictation). We have reached the stage of **drafting**. This stage, as often as not, coincides with our need to explore and as far as possible fix the overall shape of whatever we are writing. We may therefore prefer to begin by jotting down chapter headings or paragraph topics before starting to draft what we want to say in detail. Pen and paper do this better, in my experience, than a word-processor, where the limitations of the screen render large-scale structure hard to monitor and control. Intentions do not always come to fruition, as Byron insinuates:

> My poem's epic, and is meant to be
>   Divided in twelve books; each book containing
> With love, and war, a heavy gale at sea,
>   A list of ships, and captains, and kings reigning,
> New characters; the episodes are three:
>   A panoramic view of hell's in training,
> After the style of Virgil and of Homer,
> So that the name of Epic's no misnomer.[13]

But we also draft our writing in detail, trying out one set of words after another until we have sufficiently clarified our meaning – for our readers and probably for ourselves as well. This detailed wording, as it emerges, will certainly modify whatever structure we originally planned; much of the art of drafting, in fact, consists of controlling and disciplining the parts and proportions of the piece and eventually integrating them into a living, harmonious and probably unexpected whole – somewhat as my daughters, after growing up through various phases of legginess and awkwardness, became the poised and balanced people they are today. For an account of the problems posed by this stage of the writing we may again turn to Gibbon, whose comments are the more unexpected – and, for most of us, reassuring – in view of the lapidary polish of his finished product:

> No sooner was I settled in my house and library, than I undertook the composition of the first volume of my *History*. At the outset all was dark and doubtful; even the title of the work, the true era of the *Decline and Fall of the Empire*, the limits of the introduction, the division of the chapters, and the order of the narrative; and I was often tempted to cast away the labour of seven years. The style of an author should be the image of his mind, but the choice and command of language is the fruit of exercise. Many experiments were made before I could hit the middle tone between a dull chronicle and a rhetorical declamation: three times did I compose the first chapter, and twice the second and third, before I was tolerably satisfied with their effect. In the remainder of the way I advanced with a more equal and easy pace; but the fifteenth and sixteenth chapters have been reduced by three successive revisals from a large volume to their present size; and they might still be compressed, without any loss of facts or sentiment.[14]

Perhaps Gibbon might have avoided some of the trouble that beset him if he had started by *discussing* his ideas aloud with some intelligent and sympathetic listener.

His drafting in fact necessitated a good deal of **revision** (the stages of the writing process again overlap). Many writers find this the most rewarding, even exhilarating, activity:

> I forget who started the notion of my writing a series of Anglo-Indian tales, but I remember our council over the naming of the series. They were originally much longer than when they appeared, but the shortening of them, first to my own fancy after rapturous re-readings, and next to the space available, taught me that a tale from which pieces have been raked out is like a fire that has been poked. One does not know that the operation has been performed, but every one feels the effect. Note, though, that the excised stuff must have been honestly written for inclusion. I found that when, to save trouble, I 'wrote short' *ab initio* much salt went out of the work
> . . .
> This leads me to the Higher Editing. Take of well-ground Indian ink as much as suffices and a camel-hair brush proportionate to the interspaces of your lines. In an auspicious hour, read your final draft and consider faithfully every paragraph, sentence and word, blacking out where requisite. Let it lie by to drain as long as possible. At the end of that time, re-read and you should find that it will bear a second shortening. Finally, read it aloud alone and at leisure. Maybe a shade more brush work will then indicate or impose itself. If not, praise Allah and let it go, and 'when thou hast done, repent not.' The shorter the tale, the longer the brushwork and, normally, the shorter the lie-by, and *vice versa*. The longer the tale, the less brush but the longer lie-by. I have had tales by me for three or five years which shortened themselves almost yearly. The magic lies in the Brush and the Ink. For the Pen, when it is writing, can only scratch; and bottled ink is not to compare with the ground Chinese stick. *Experto crede.*[15]

P. G. Wodehouse, most prolific and disciplined of twentieth-century writers of fiction, endorses this passage in a letter to his friend Bill Townend:

> Did you read Kipling's autobiography? In that he maintains that the principal thing in writing is to cut. Somerset Maugham says the same. Kipling says it's like raking slag out of a fire to make the fire burn brighter. I know just what he means. You can skip as you read, but if the superfluous stuff is there, it affects you just the same. The trouble is to know where to cut. I generally find with my own stuff that it's unnecessary lines in the dialogue that are wrong, but then my books are principally dialogue.[16]

Beatrix Potter concurs about the importance of cutting, adding some comments that may prompt us to view her writing through new eyes:

> I think I write carefully because I enjoy my writing, and enjoy taking pains over it. I have always disliked writing to order; I write to please myself . . . My usual way of writing is to scribble, and cut out, and write it again and again. The shorter and plainer the better. And read the Bible (unrevised version and Old Testament) if I feel my style wants chastening.[17]

But revision entails alteration as well as cutting, as we search for the 'right' words. As library collections of writers' manuscript material accumulate so the opportunities for studying their habits of revision proliferate. Robert Graves' emendations to the last stanza of his poem *To Juan at the Winter Solstice* stand as a good example. Its final published form runs:

> Dwell on her graciousness, dwell on her smiling,
> Do not forget what flowers
> The great boar trampled down in ivy time.
> Her brow was creamy as the crested wave,
> Her sea-blue eyes were wild
> But nothing promised that is not performed.[18]

Graves' manuscripts show the development of this stanza from some very different original rough ideas through a penultimate version which reads:

> Dwell on her graciousness, dwell on her smiling,
> Never forget what flowers
> A wild-boar trampled down in ivy time.
> Her brow was whiter than the long ninth wave, ·
> Her sea-blue eyes were wild
> And nothing promised that is not performed.[19]

The differences are instructive: Graves' final version rejects the slightly hectoring tone of "never forget," foregrounds the boar, prefers alliteration (*creamy . . . crested*) to assonance (*whiter . . . ninth*) in the fourth line (while removing the puzzling irrelevance of *ninth*), and ends on a note of contrast (*But . . .*) rather than of accretion (*And . . .*). Nevertheless the poet probably makes most of these alterations, as most of us do, simply because they *feel right* – as indeed a careful reading confirms.

Revision of any kind thus demands full alertness. But cuts in particular, as the metaphor implies, may hurt; as a result they usually demand self-discipline, and may indeed bear testimony to the "unshakeable courage" which we saw Lauris Edmond attributing to the "great poets" in Chapter 1.[20] Mark Twain, for example, excised a passage of more than five thousand words from Chapter 14 of *Huckleberry Finn* – all good, stirring stuff, full of action and including a ghost story – in the interests of economy and relevance. [21] Whatever its perils, however, revision rarely becomes boring.

Unfortunately, few writers would say the same of **proofreading**:

> Oh I am so tired of correcting my own writing – these 8 articles – I have however learnt I think to dash: not to finick. I mean the writing is free enough: it's the repulsiveness of correcting that nauseates me . . . I finished my re-typing of *The Waves*. Not that it is finished – oh dear no. For then I must correct the re-re-typing . . . O to seek relief from this incessant correction . . .[22]

Six hundred years before Virginia Woolf thus lamented, Geoffrey Chaucer had had much the same problems with his copyist (*scriveyn*) Adam:

> Adam scriveyn, if ever it thee befalle
> *Boece* or *Troylus* for to wryten newe.
> Under thy long lokkes thou most have the scalle,
> But after my makyng thow wryte more trewe;
> So ofte a-daye I mot thy werk renewe
> It to correcte and eek to rubbe and scrape;
> And al is thorugh thy negligence and rape.[23]

Perhaps because of the tedious and mechanical labour it demands, proofreading seems to be the point at which writers' morale and critical self-assessment slump to their lowest levels:

> Here a word. As I re-read *At the Bay* in proof, it seemed to me flat, dull, and not a success at all. I was very much ashamed of it. I am.[24]

At this stage of writing there nevertheless seems no way to escape the need to "correct the re-re-typing" or – if we are working with quill pen and parchment – "to rubbe and scrape". The word-processor, already invaluable for purposes of revision, saves much paper and physical labour during proof-reading but should not seduce us into the inattention that so easily besets us. Try as we may, familiarity blinds us to many of the solecisms in what we have written, with the result that a different pair of eyes will probably do a better job. Failing that, a lapse of time helps, while tricks like reading aloud, covering the next line with a ruler, or starting at the last sentence and working forwards one sentence at a time all help to isolate errors. We must define these, of course, as 'things we didn't mean to write – a notion that sheds light both on *the writer's intention* as discussed in Chapter 3 and on *correctness* as discussed in Chapter 4. Both Woolf and Chaucer use the verb 'to correct' in the sense of 'to bring into line with the purposes of the author' (rather than of 'the dictionary' or any other exterior authority). In spite of its tedium, proofreading thus plays a valuable and necessary part in the writing process.

It also foreshadows **publication,** which both justifies the rigours of proof-reading and consummates our original purpose in writing – whether exploratory, pragmatic, personal, social, aesthetic, anecdotal, political or, as is most common, some inextricable mixture of all these. We may use the term to cover all the means by which a piece of writing reaches an audience: mailing a letter or pushing a note under the door; pinning a notice on the board or a pupil's work on the classroom wall; submitting an essay or thesis; printing a newspaper article or report; hoisting a banner; sending a manuscript to a publisher; and so on and so on. This too takes its place as a normal part of the process of writing, and exercises powerful influence on all the other stages as they occur; as we saw in Chapter 3, our awareness of our audience contributes significantly to what we have to say and to the way we say it. Publication therefore matters, whether or not the piece of writing concerned ever reaches its intended audience. And even a private diary presumably addresses our future selves:

> I never travel without my diary. One should always have something sensational to read in the train.[25]

The foregoing account of the writing process, with its artificial division into six 'stages', clearly fails to mention much of importance in the actual experience of writing. This experience, equally clearly, varies enormously from one writer to the next:

> Let us now consider the Personal Daemon of Aristotle and others, of whom it has been truthfully written, though not published:-
>
> > This is the doom of the Makers – their Daemon lives in their pen.
> > If he be absent or sleeping, they are even as other men.
> > But if he be utterly present. and they swerve not from his behest.
> > The word that he gives shall continue. whether in earnest or jest.
>
> Most men, and some most unlikely, keep him under an alias which varies

with their literary or scientific attainments. Mine came to me early when I sat bewildered among other notions, and said: 'Take this and no other.' I obeyed, and was rewarded . . . My Daemon was with me in the *Jungle Books*, *Kim* and both Puck books, and good care I took to walk delicately, lest he should withdraw. I know that he did not, because when those books were finished they said so themselves with, almost, the water-hammer click of a tap turned off. One of the clauses in our contract was that I should never follow up 'a success,' for by this sin fell Napoleon and a few others. *Note here.* When your Daemon is in charge, do not try to think consciously. Drift, wait, and obey.[26]

The experience Rudyard Kipling thus recounts compares interestingly with that of George Orwell:

All writers are vain, selfish, and lazy, and at the very bottom of their motives there lies a mystery. Writing a book is a horrible, exhausting struggle, like a long bout of some painful illness. One would never undertake such a thing if one were not driven on by some demon whom one can neither resist nor understand. For all one knows that demon is simply the same instinct that makes a baby squall for attention. And yet it is also true that one can write nothing readable unless one constantly struggles to efface one's own personality. Good prose is like a windowpane.[27]

And with both these prose accounts we may compare a piece of poetry (likely therefore to make its point more accurately) by Ted Hughes:

> I imagine this midnight moment's forest:
> Something else is alive
> Beside the clock's loneliness
> And this blank page where my fingers move.
>
> Through the window I see no star:
> Something more near
> Though deeper within darkness
> Is entering the loneliness:
>
> Cold, delicately as the dark snow,
> A fox's nose touches twig, leaf;
> Two eyes serve a movement, that now
> And again now, and now, and now
>
> Sets neat prints into the snow
> Between trees, and warily a lame
> Shadow lags by stump and in hollow
> Of a body that is bold to come

Across clearings, an eye,
A widening deepening greenness,
Brilliantly, concentratedly,
Coming about its own business

Till, with a sudden sharp hot stink of fox
It enters the dark hole of the head.
The window is starless still; the clock ticks,
The page is printed.[28]

Daemon, demon or *fox, window* or *tap,* the metaphors grope hesitantly towards the unutterable. All witnesses seem to agree, however, that in one way or another the writing process can endanger your health. It can also, on the other hand, bring astonishing rewards:

A note to say I am all trembling with pleasure — can't go on with my Letter — because Harold Nicholson has rung up to say *The Waves* is a masterpiece. Ah Hah — so it wasn't all wasted then.[29]

Notes

1 Koestler p. 40
2 Woolf pp. 165-6
3 Herrick p. 58
4 Borrow pp. 43-7
5 Frye p. 17
6 Hazlitt Vol. 17, p. 119 *My First Acquaintance with Poets*
7 see Malcolm Cowley in Ghiselin pp. 148-9
8 Kipling vol. XXIV p. 517
9 Hopkins p. 114
10 Boswell p. 466
11 Gibbon p. 98. *Disgusted* carried less force in the eighteenth century than today; a modern equivalent would be *disenchanted.*
12 Gibbon p. 94
13 Byron *Don Juan* I, CC
14 Gibbon pp. 97-8
15 Kipling pp. 501-2. *Ab initio* = from the beginning. *Experto crede* = believe one who has proved it.
16 Wodehouse p. 158
17 letter to Bertha Mahoney, quoted in Lane p.150
18 Graves p. 200
19 cf. Croft, Vol. II, pp. 183-4
20 cf. p. 12

21 see Twain pp. 371-84. Nothing need ever be lost for good: Twain later incorporated the passage into *Life on the Mississippi.*
22 Woolf pp. 170-1
23 Chaucer p. 650
24 Mansfield pp. 196-7
25 Wilde, Oscar *The Importance of Being Ernest* Act II
26 Kipling pp. 502-3
27 Orwell *England Your England* p. 15
28 Hughes p. 14
29 Woolf p. 175

8

THE DEVELOPMENT OF WRITING

Why doth this generation seek after a sign?
Mark 10:13

Some knowledge of how writing has developed, and of how that development has reflected things like technology and social conditions, will further our understanding of many of the issues – particularly those connected with mimesis and meaning – that we examined in earlier chapters. Besides this, some notion of the sheer age and venerability of the signs we use will encourage us to treat them with the respect they merit. In this chapter therefore we will trace briefly, and with a good deal of over-simplification and some incidental discussion of the underlying issues, the enormously complex evolution of written signs from their earliest **pictographic** forms, through the **ideograms** and **phonograms** that grew out of these and gave way in turn, to the **alphabetical** system that English and many (though by no means all) other languages use as a visual equivalent to the spoken word today.

In doing so, we will inevitably use words like *development* (as in the title of this chapter), *evolution, growth* and so on. But we should resist any connotations these words possess that might suggest that what has happened to writing over the centuries has been systematic or shaped by any kind of pattern or purpose; still less should we conclude that methods of writing, or the societies adopting them, have steadily become better and better with the passage of time. We will court less danger of being hoodwinked by our own arrogance if we assume that writing like everything else, simply changes – and that societies turn to the kind of writing, as they adopt the kind of language, best suited to their needs, aspirations and convenience: although today the western world writes alphabetically, recent developments in international co-operation like the European Common Market have prompted a remarkable resurgence of ideographic sign-systems embodying directions for laundering garments, working the controls of a car, navigating that car across a given stretch of landscape, and so on. And for all the incidental benefits of science and technology few of us would be bold enough to claim any *absolute* superiority for the twentieth century A.D. over any of its predecessors, or for our own culture over any of its siblings.

The human race has of course been drawing pictures and carving artefacts since long before it can remember. Though the detailed purposes of many prehistoric examples must remain a partial mystery to us, such representations seem fully to have served the communicative needs – presumably religious, ritual and aesthetic as well as practical – of 'hunter-gatherer' systems of economy. Some may have been produced as long as 30,000 years ago, they seem to have occurred in all parts of the world, and they remain in widespread use. In so far as such creations store and convey information we may regard them as forms of writing. They operate in two ways in particular: as marks of ownership or identity (like cattle-brands and the modern logo) and as aids to memory (like rosaries or *he rakau whakapapa*, the notched and carved wooden boards that hold the key to Maori genealogies).

Only with the development of a settled agriculture and the trade that accompanies it did there arise the need for some portable, adaptable and reasonably permanent system of conventions for storing information and recording human transactions – for writing as we generally think of it. It may be worth noting here that the entire technology of writing – from its earliest operations in wet clay to the latest refinements of the word-processor – has developed in response to the needs of business rather than to those of literature. Literature began, and long continued, as an oral, unwritten phenomenon and has only very recently – within the last two or three hundred years, in fact – accommodated itself securely to its written environment. Many indeed would argue that it has never fully done so, and probably never will; as this book has hinted from time to time, some tension between the demands of speech and the demands of writing remains a fundamental condition of the business of writing.

In response to the demands of commerce, the earliest full writing systems developed sometime around or after 3,500 B.C. in various parts of the Middle East, from the Nile valley to that of the Indus in what is now Pakistan. They took various forms. From about 3,000 B.C. onwards Egyptian hieroglyphic script enjoyed a long and colourful history, generating an elegant and complex *hieratic* (priestly) form for religious and commemorative purposes as well as a simpler and more manageable *demotic* (popular) form for trade. In the valley of the Indus appeared another script, extant today in small quantities and still undeciphered. Scholars have so far been unable to determine whether or not this or possibly some other Middle Eastern writing system eventually made its way around 2,000 B.C. into Indo-China and hence into China proper as the ancestor of modern Chinese and Japanese writing, or whether this developed independently, as presumably did the scripts of pre-Columban Central and South America from sometime after 1,000 B.C.

Either or both of the Egyptian and Indian scripts may have been developed from that used in the fertile crescent of Mesopotamia around and between the valleys of the rivers Tigris and Euphrates. This, the remotest recorded ancestor of the script you are reading at the moment, we call *cuneiform* (meaning wedge-shaped) because it consisted of marks impressed into soft clay by means of a small metal wedge. Years of patient scholarship have established the history and characteristics of this script as well as of the Sumerian culture that used it. It began as a largely **pictographic** script – a kind of writing whose characters purport to depict the concrete objects in the world around. This independence from language of course renders the script intelligible to readers who may not otherwise be able to communicate with each other – as modern Chinese writing serves all the speakers of the many mutually unintelligible dialects of that language. But, also like modern Chinese writing, such a script necessarily contains an enormous number of complex characters to be learnt – characters as numerous as the things the writer wants to write about. As long ago as the early seventeenth century Francis Bacon drew all this to the attention of the western world as evidence for his conclusions about the relationship between language and ideas:

> For the organ of tradition [i.e. of communication], it is either speech or writing: for Aristotle saith well, 'Words are the images of cogitations, and letters are the images of words.' But yet it is not of necessity that cogitations be expressed by the medium of words. For whatsoever is capable of sufficient differences, and those perceptible by the sense, is in nature competent to express cogitations. And therefore we see in the commerce of barbarous people, that understand not one another's language, and in the practice of divers that are dumb and deaf, that men's minds are expressed in gestures, though not exactly, yet to serve the turn. And we understand further, that it is the use of China, and the kingdoms of the High Levant, to write in characters real, which express neither letters or words in gross, but things or notions; insomuch as countries and provinces, which understand not one another's language, can nevertheless read one another's writings, because the characters are accepted more generally than the languages do extend; and

therefore they have a vast multitude of characters, as many (I suppose) as radical words.[1]

But even the most elaborately pictographic writing cannot represent the world in full or with total precision: the drawing of an ox or a bird inevitably conveys not only the particular individual of that species that you may be planning to buy or sell but also the *idea* of 'ox' or 'bird' in general. In acknowledgement of this, few pictograms attempt to draw the entire object or to do so with full realism: early scripts usually represented an ox merely by a front view of its face and horns. All pictographic scripts, that is to say, already represent reality with some degree of abstraction, and in fact consist of ready-made **ideograms**, 'pictures of ideas' (or of what Bacon calls *notions*). The idea of *bird* can readily extend to cover the idea of *flight*, while the pictogram for the sun will easily suggest notions of *day* or *light* and so on. As time passed, therefore, cuneiform script increasingly exploited its inbuilt ideographic qualities, achieving greater efficiency and practicality by conventionalizing its characters and substantially reducing their number as, by an essentially metaphoric process, different aspects of the world were observed to share basically identical underlying ideas.

Both pictographic and ideographic scripts share one important quality, however. Both are **semasiographic** (consisting of 'signs for things' – whether objects or ideas) unlike our **glottographic** English script today, which consists largely of 'signs for words' (though we have always relied on ideograms for our system of numerals, for mathematical and musical symbols and for handy everyday signs like $, £, %, &, ®, # and so on). Fundamental differences obviously exist between these two kinds of writing system, and the move from the first to the second presents writers, and the scholars who chronicle their progress, with enormous problems.

Cuneiform writing seems to have acquired some glottographic qualities before falling into disuse with the decline of the societies that fostered it and the rise of alternative writing systems. Since the human voice can only utter a limited number of sounds and combinations of sound, certain utterances are bound to acquire several meanings; thus we articulate the sound *led* to mean a heavy metal as well as the past form of the verb *to lead*. Accidental similarities of this kind may result in many a spelling mistake, and probably in many a pun, but they seem unavoidable. Users of cuneiform script noticed and exploited such homonyms. Their word for *arrow*, for instance, *ti*, happened also to be their word for *life*: the arrow-ideogram (simply the conventionalized picture of an arrow) therefore served to represent the word *life*, and in due course, by a reasonable extension, to suggest the sound *ti* wherever it occured. The ideogram has thus become a **phonogram**, representing a sound rather than a thing or idea of a thing, and the movement to glottography has begun. We see the same thing still happening when people put notices saying '4-sale' in their car windows; and to join two such phonograms together – as we might juxtapose pictures of a bee and a leaf to make the word *belief* – is called a *rebus device*.

This seems to be about as far as cuneiform writing went, leaving the various scripts that replaced it to inch further in the direction of full glottography. The second millenium B.C. saw the rise in the Middle East of various Semitic scripts. No one knows for sure how far these represented developments from older writing-systems or how far they had been invented from scratch. The most important of them (in retrospect) were: Hebrew, in which the bulk of the Old Testament of the Bible is written; Aramaic, the script of the speech of Jesus and of the remaining parts of the Old Testament, ancestor of the scripts of modern India and South-east Asia and (via Nabataean) of modern Arabic writing; and Phoenician, which, widely used for purposes of trade around the Mediterranean basin, was eventually adapted by the Greeks into the world's first fully *alphabetical* writing system. The Greek alphabet was certainly in existence by the eighth century B.C., the date of the earliest alphabetical inscriptions so far unearthed. From the Greek system in turn came, eventually, scripts like Cyrillic (the script of modern Russian and a great many other Slavonic languages) and the Etruscan alphabet of Italy which itself gave rise to the Roman form, adapted in due course by our English-speaking ancestors into the script you are reading at the moment.

Exactly how the phonographic Semitic scripts and their offspring modulated into full alphabeticism remains hard to trace. A phonographic script remains *syllabic*, producing a separate symbol to match each syllable of speech, or, like the Semitic scripts, *consonantal*, suggesting the consonants of each syllable but giving little guidance about the pronunciation of vowels. The Hebrew *tetragrammaton*, the divine Name composed of four phonograms and widely considered too holy to utter, which we may show in English script as JHWH, presents characteristic problems; transliterated in the King James version of the Bible as Jehovah, it occurs in twentieth century translations as Yahweh (unless rendered The Lord, which solves the problem by dodging it). Various Semitic scripts seem to have tried, by means of various systems of marks, to indicate vowel sounds, but never with lasting success.

Scholarly debate continues over how separate and permanent signs for the vowels (**a, e, i, o, u**, and sometimes **y**) came into existence. Some have suggested the principle of *acrophony* (from the Greek word for *top* or *tip* – cf. acrobat, acronym, Acropolis etc.). By this principle a pictogram or ideogram comes to represent the initial sound of the word for whatever it depicts. Thus the Hebrew ideogram for an ox comes to represent the vowel /**a**/ because the Hebrew word for ox (*aleph*) begins with that sound – and, in theory at least, a vowel is born. It is not, unfortunately, as simple as that, because *aleph* in Hebrew script in fact represents not a vowel but that consonant for which English script has no specific sign but which we know as the glottal stop. This sound occurs in the back of the throat and is substituted in certain English dialects (like cockney) for the letter t following a vowel ("Wo' a lo' of glo'al stops!"). But a vowel certainly emerged in due course, with its Greek name *alpha* suggesting some indebtedness to Hebrew antecedents. And we may be tempted to turn our capital A upside down and fancy that we can see the face of the ox still staring ruminatively at us. The principle of acrophony, if valid, can of course operate across different languages (since that is what pictograms and ideograms do). The Semitic writing systems probably developed their consonant signs from Egyptian hieroglyphs by some such process. Runes, those mysterious and evocative Scandinavian letters, may also have evolved acrophonically from ancient pictograms, though they owe something as well to the Roman script and its descendants.

The Roman alphabet originally contained only twenty-one letters, distinguished from their Greek counterparts mainly by their preference for curves instead of straight lines: **S** for Σ, **D** for Δ and so on. The number has fluctuated since, in response to the varying needs of the various languages for which it has been adapted. English, for example, has found it convenient to distinguish **i** from **j** and **y**, and **v** from **u** and **w**. The Roman letters have also appeared in a wide variety of shapes as different styles of handwriting have flourished, especially before the introduction of the printing-press, with forms like the uncial and half-uncial of the late Roman empire, Carolingian miniscule, the elaborate and beautiful (though sometimes rather heavy) Gothic of the high Middle Ages, the Antiqua of the Renaissance and its more recent Italic successor. This last, a partially cursive script, stands as the immediate ancestor of the way we write in manuscript today, though even that remains unsettled: you can guess at people's ages by the way they write the letter **r**. Most modern type-face, on the other hand, enshrines the conventions of Antiqua, as we can see by the shape of its **a** as compared with the *a* of Italic-based manuscripts.

The conventions of writing have in fact varied enormously over the millenia. As we saw in Chapter 3, leaving spaces between words is a relatively modern habit. The bulk of ancient writing either dispenses with spacing altogether, or attempts to separate words by means of marks such as lines or dots just as my word-processor does when I give it the appropriate instruction. *Plus ça change, plus c'est la même chose.* Nor of course has all writing followed the left-to-right and top-to-bottom order that we so readily take for granted (and seems so deeply implanted in our consciousness that some producers of plays always bring a ghost on stage from the audience's right in order to run counter to 'normal' expectations). Many modern scripts of course run from right to left (Hebrew and Arabic, for example), while Chinese and Japanese often run vertically from top to bottom. In the history of writing almost every other possible order has been used, in every possible combination of left to right, right to left, top to bottom and bottom to top. Ancient writing, including Greek, frequently followed the *boustrophedon* system ('as the ox ploughs')

> working along one line as an ox-plough drives in a furrow, and
> .noitcerid etisoppo eht ni kcab gninrut neht

Some boustrophedon writing even reversed the symbols (after the fashion of Lewis Carroll's looking-glass writing) as well as the line direction. Other scripts have been written in circles, or spirals, or even in totally random distribution (it being part of the scribal mystery to know which part to go to next).

Writing systems thus reflect the assumptions, economy and ethos of the societies that produce them, providing the level and kind of information storage each society requires. A pictographic or ideographic system will best serve the needs of a loosely organized culture concerned with the daily demands of survival, particularly where small groups speaking different languages or dialects need to communicate or trade with each other. Such a system will also reflect its society's metaphysics, where physical and natural objects are seen as mysterious and valuable in their own right without the need for further analysis, abstraction or classification. The society will, in our terms, use magic rather than science, its religion will tend to be ancestral and animistic rather than deistic, its characteristic literary form will be epic and its literary mode oral.

A society that produces a surplus, on the other hand, will generate property and the complex social organization that inevitably accompanies it. This comprises things like politics, law, administration and enforcement agencies, and concomitants like science and speculative theology. All these activities not only demand information storage of a very efficient and quickly retrievable kind but depend heavily on language for their operations. They will therefore demand and generate writing systems of the glottographic or phonetic sort, which will record the language itself rather than attempting to enshrine whatever 'reality' stands behind the language, sacrificing universality in writing for efficiency, but probably seeking to rediscover some form of universal truth through processes of abstraction and metaphor. Indeed the preoccupations of such a society will probably centre upon the kinds of topic – mimesis and so on – discussed in the first seven chapters of this book and explored profoundly and lovingly by linguistic scholars like Ernest Fenollosa in terms not only revealing the writer's 'realism' (cf. Chapter 1) but surprisingly reminiscent of the statement by Francis Bacon we quoted above:

> Perhaps we do not always sufficiently consider that thought is successive, not through some accident or weakness of our subjective operations but because the operations of nature are successive. The transferences of force from agent to object which constitute natural phenomena occupy time. Therefore a reproduction of them in imagination requires the same temporal order.
>
> Suppose we look out of a window and watch a man. Suddenly he turns his head and actively fixes his attention upon something. We look ourselves and see that his vision has been focussed upon a horse. We saw, first, the man before he acted; second, while he acted; third, the object toward which his action was directed. In speech we split up the rapid continuity of this action and of its picture into its three essential parts or joints in the right order, and say:
>
> Man sees horse.
>
> It is clear that these three joints, or words, are only three phonetic symbols, which stand for the three terms of a natural process. But we could quite as easily denote these three stages of our thought by symbols equally arbitrary, *which had no basis in sound*: for example by three Chinese characters:

| Man | Sees | Horse |

> If we all knew *what division* of this mental horse-picture each of these signs stood for, we could communicate continuous thought to one another as

easily by drawing them as by speaking words. We habitually employ the visible language of gesture in much this same manner.

But Chinese notation is something much more than arbitrary symbols. It is based upon a vivid shorthand picture of the operations of nature. In the algebraic figure and in the spoken word there is no natural connection between thing and sign: all depends upon sheer convention. But the Chinese method follows natural suggestion. First stands a man on his two legs. Second, his eye moves through space: a bold figure represented by running legs but unforgettable once you have seen it. Third stands the horse on his four legs.

The thought picture is not only called up by these signs as well as by words but far more vividly and concretely. Legs belong to all three characters: they are *alive*. The group holds something of the quality of a continuous moving picture.[2]

Fenollosa's insights remind us that western society as a whole has lost as well as gained by turning from semasiographic to glottographic script in general. The power of such visual images may well in part account for the recent resurgence of ideographs we noticed earlier.

There seems little doubt that, in the emergence of writing systems, art imitates life in that social conditions produce the systems they need. Life will continue to imitate art, of course, in so far as the things people write offer new visions to their readers. But, as we saw at the beginning of this chapter, literature has usually been slow to adjust to the technological changes and innovations produced in response to social pressures like trade and war. Thus Tennyson, after inspecting a railway for the first time, though moved to exclaim

> Forward, forward let us range,
> Let the great world spin for ever down the ringing grooves of change

learnt only later that trains ran not in *grooves* but on rails.[3]

The enormous technological changes in writing have come about for much the same reason as the writing systems themselves, and the two appear very difficult to disentangle. Clearly some of the early methods of writing that seem so slow and ponderous to us – using a chisel to impress marks in wet clay or to engrave them in stone – suited the static nature of the societies that practised them, with their strong emphasis on permanence, durability and even eternity. Equally clearly the use of papyrus, the reed-brush and ink suited the increasing pace and size of trade and political life in the second and first millenia B.C. and facilitated the development of more cursive demotic scripts. Vellum (parchment) and the quill-pen combined permanence with portability in a way that suited the economic and cultural needs of the later Roman empire with its long distances and wide climatic range. And manuscripts made with these materials enabled the Christian church to preserve much of what it felt to be of permanent value through the subsequent centuries of cultural and political disruption.

The most influential writing material of all, paper, had been developed by the Chinese sometime before the second century A.D. It reached Europe, by way of the Arabs, a thousand years later, and demonstrated much of the durability of vellum while proving much easier to write on. It has ruled the world for almost a millenium, stimulating the invention of a variety of tools for writing on it in place of the brush or the quill-pen – the metal nib, the typewriter, the ball-point pen and so on. Above all, it made feasible the development, by Johann Gutenberg in the fifteenth century, of the movable-type printing-press with its inconceivably profound influence, for better or worse, on every aspect of human life. Only in recent years, perhaps as we have come to realize that the world contains too many people and too few trees, have alternative methods of storing information started to rival paper. Photographic and electronic techniques will certainly stimulate changes in our writing systems at least as revolutionary as those that we have surveyed in this chapter.

This survey should remind us that the writing system we choose (and most of us have comparatively little choice) itself makes some pretty fundamental statements about what the world is like and about how we see ourselves as fitting into it. By using, as I do and must, an alphabetical system I inevitably assent to the social and metaphysical – even theological – assumptions that such a system serves. Writing, I imply, imitates words, and words, as you will have gathered, play the leading role in my scenario of how the world operates. *In the beginning was the Word.* All this of course reinforces the suggestion we made in Chapter 1 that the conventions of our writing – the words and structures we inherit and use – play a far more important part than we usually realize in establishing and conveying our meaning. To fly a philosophical kite for a moment, we may postulate an enormous, perhaps infinite, number of statements we are quite unable to make either in speech or in writing, because we lack the wherewithal to make them and probably therefore even to conceive of them.

We should be reminded too of the unbridgeable gap that this book has postulated from time to time between language of any kind and whatever it purports to imitate. Writing of an alphabetical sort like ours, imitating speech, presumably rests at least one step further away from any material reality that speech attempts to refer to. In contrast to the picture we saw

Fenollosa painting of semasiographic writing systems (pictograms and ideograms) and the dramatic immediacy of their impact:

> sound writing (phonetic writing) is far more complex. It is not as we, on the basis of our own experience and training might be tempted to assume, more natural, nor even necessarily more effective. In many ways it is a tortuous and somewhat unnatural process. An idea has to be translated first into the sounds of a particular word or sentence in a particular language, then those sounds have to be made visible in the form of engraved, painted or incised signs on the surface of a definite object, signs which more often than not bear no relation to the content of the original thought. In order to consult the information (and ultimately the whole purpose of information storage is communication) these visual signs have to be translated back into the sounds of the same language, and from this the word, the sentence and the original idea have to be reconstructed in the mind of the reader. And this is in fact exactly how primitive people without any writing of their own view the process.[4]

We may entertain some reservations about the notion of 'idea first, words later'[5] assumed in the above statement, though with the backing of thinkers like Aristotle, Bacon, Locke, Fenollosa and Orwell it clearly deserves serious consideration. But such issues must not distract us from recognizing the magnitude of what we undertake, and indeed of what we achieve, whenever we put pen to paper or finger to keyboard.

Notes

1 Bacon p.131
2 Fenollosa pp. 7-9
3 Tennyson *Locksley Hall* 11.181-2
4 Gaur p. 15
5 see Chapter 1

9

THE HISTORY OF ENGLISH

Tell me
What is your opinion of Progress? Does it, for example,
Exist? Is there ever progression without retrogression?
Therefore is it not true that mankind
Can more justly be said increasingly to Gress?

Christopher Fry

If the English language can ever be said to have begun it presumably did so during the middle decades of the fifth century A.D. as speakers of various dialects of the Anglo-Frisian branch of Low German crossed the narrow seas to occupy a Roman-Celtic Britain largely bereft of its defences. Rome herself, under constant pressure from barbarian invaders, had been sacked by the Goths under Alaric in 410 A.D., while Slavs, Huns, Vandals and others continued to make inroads leading to the final collapse of the western Empire in 476 A.D. Not surprisingly, the tottering establishment had little thought, money or military aid to spare for the remote and unimportant islands on its margins, which could only attempt to stem their share of the barbarian tide by mustering a mobile cavalry force under the command of an individual who may have achieved later immortality as Arthur of Britain; what little we know of events in fifth century Britain remains shrouded in hearsay, legend and political propaganda, all accumulating into myth.

No language begins from scratch, however, and we may well wonder whence these Anglo-Saxon invaders and their languages had come. Historians, archeologists, comparative linguists and others searching for an answer to this question point us to an astonishing series of population movements, over a period of several thousand years, apparently originating from the vast and comparatively arid grassland steppes of central Asia. The nomadic inhabitants, having domesticated the horse and mastered the use of the wheel, proceeded to move outwards, east, south and west, presumably as increases in their own population prompted them to search for a different and perhaps less harsh environment. Wave overlapped wave of this expansion, creating one of the biggest, and certainly one of the most significant, population movements the world has ever seen. Its final ripples – if it has ever really stopped – lapped Earth's furthest shores, and account among other things for the fact that I am writing this book in English while sitting in my study in New Zealand. A few drops have even reached the Moon and beyond.

Its story remains far too complicated to be described in any detail here. Eastward it reached into northern Tibet, southward into the Indian sub-continent as far as the valley of the Indus, and westward in a series of powerful surges into Europe and beyond. Since, in the early stages at least, many of these population groups were illiterate, and since few of them while on the move left much in the way of durable artefacts and inscriptions, language provides much of the evidence for what we know or guess. In 1786 Sir William Jones, while serving as a judge in British India, learnt to read Sanskrit, the linguistic ancestor of modern Hindi, written examples of which survive from as long ago as 1500 B.C. He found remarkable similarities between its vocabulary and those of Greek, Latin and several Germanic languages. Scholars since then have identified grammatical and syntactical parallels as well as verbal ones, and have added a great many more languages to the list, classifying them as the Indo-European group or family.

Many such families exist – the Semitic (including Hebrew and Arabic); the Ural-Altaic (including languages as widely separated as Turkish and Mongolian); the Finno-Ugraic (Finnish, Hungarian); the Sino-Tibetan (including Chinese); the Dravidian (Tamil and various other languages of South India); the Malayo-Polynesian (south Pacific languages from Malayan to Maori); the Bantu of southern Africa; the Algonquian of the American Indian peoples; Papuan; Eskimo (though some scholars think this an offshoot of the Indo-European family); and many others. The language of the Basque people of the Franco-Spanish border occupies an intriguing niche of its own, demonstrating no apparent relationship to any other language in the world. Linguists have done much work identifying and classifying the members of each group and tracing the human history that each enshrines. Much remains to be done, while questions about where the groups themselves came from, with the implications such questions bear about the origin of language and of the human race itself, can at the moment arouse little more than speculation.

The Indo-European group (once called the Aryan, until the Nazi party gave that word a bad name) has been intensively studied, and scholars know much about how its members are related. In Chapter 1 we saw Ernest Fenollosa tracing the Aryan roots of the common English words *is* and *be*. As long ago as the eighteenth century Jacob and Wilhelm Grimm, compilers of Grimm's fairy-tales, formulated *Grimm's Law* to account for consonantal differences within the group. From all the accumulated evidence we may deduce the conditions under which early Indo-European language speakers lived: many of the group's member-languages share words, clearly of great antiquity, for the flora and fauna of temperate grasslands. The English *ewe*, for example (Old English *eowu*), common in Germanic languages (including those of Scandinavia) as the generic term for sheep, occurs as *ouis* in Latin and equally recognizably in Greek, Old Iranian, Old Slavonic, Lithuanian and Sanskrit. Words for horse, wolf, wind, sky and yoke are equally widely distributed, as are some terms of kinship (English *father*, German *vater*, Latin *pater*, Sanskrit *piter*), numerals, pronouns and some forms of verb-modification. No trace, significantly, exists of common terms for things connected with the sea or the tropics.

A simplified 'family tree' to show where English takes its place among a representative sample of the Indo-European group of languages looks something like this (the asterisk after the parent-language indicates its hypothetical status):

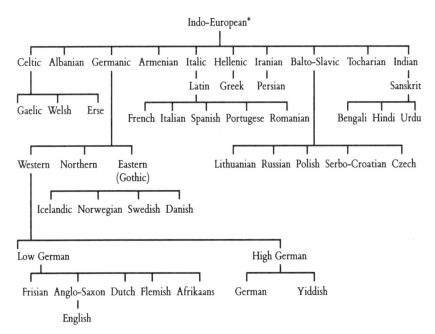

This diagram, for all its breadth, fails to suggest how our horse-riding, sheep and cattle-herding, wagon and chariot-mounted linguistic ancestors spread westward from their windswept homelands into Europe, usually fighting each step of the way, conquering either the aboriginal inhabitants of the land or – as did the Romans, Anglo-Saxons, Danes and Normans in Britain – their own Indo-European predecessors, and eventually imposing their languages on the whole continent except for Finland, Hungary and the Basque country. The diagram also ignores important ancient members of the family like the Hittite and Illyrian languages, and mobile ones like Romany, the languages of the Gypsies. Its speakers originated in India, whence, more than a thousand years ago, they moved via Persia into much of Europe and beyond, keeping their language, culture and identity largely intact to this day. Their often unwilling European hosts attributed to them a variety of origins: the English called them *Egyptians* (*Gypsies*), the French *Bohemians*, the Swedes *Tartars*, the Spanish *Flemings* (*Flamencos*), and the Germans and Dutch simply *Heathen*; while their language was attributed to Romania.

When in discussing the origins of English we speak of a *family-tree* of Indo-European languages and use cognate terms like *ancestor*, *parent-language* and so on we should never forget that we are using metaphors, and that, as we saw in Chapter 2, we are likely as a result to create some distortion as well as clarification. This particular metaphor distorts because, unlike a human being, a language does not die (unless some cataclysm wipes out all its speakers, all its records and everyone likely to learn from them). To call Latin 'a dead language' distorts the truth, because Latin did not die; it changed with time and circumstances and remains alive and well under a variety of different names – Italian, French, Spanish and so on. In some ways we speak today – and I am writing in this book – the very language that emerged from the steppes of Russia so long ago. Of course a few changes have occurred; they always do, and are still happening. A single decade is enough to observe the process, and several hundred decades will change a language out of all recognition. But it remains the same language. Much of this chapter will summarize the changes that have taken place in our particular version of Indo-European since our rather arbitrary starting-point in the middle of the fifth century.

Tradition groups the Anglo-Saxon invaders of the fifth century into three groups: the Angles, who took the north; the Saxons, who took the south; and the Jutes, who settled in Kent under their formidable leaders Hengist and Horsa. Probably the reality was not as tidy as that: certainly the major Saxon kingdoms – Wessex, Middlesex, Sussex and Essex of the west, middle, south and east Saxons respectively – appeared around and south of the river Thames, while the Angles took East Anglia and parts of the north. But the Jutes must remain hypothetical. Whatever they called themselves, the new arrivals united in classifying the previous occupants as *wealas* (*foreigners*, and the source of our word *Welsh*) and driving them into the more rugged western areas of the country.

As the new occupants settled down and, through contact with the Irish and Roman churches, adopted Christianity along with a substantial vocabulary of Latin-derived words like *bishop, school, library* and *medicine*, sophisticated cultures flourished – in Northumbria in the seventh century, Mercia (in the centre of the country) in the eighth, and in the south in Alfred's Wessex during the ninth. This last proved a bastion of resistance against yet another wave of Indo-European invasion, as from the mid-ninth century onwards the Danes invaded, eventually taking over much of England north of the Thames (the Danelaw) and contributing yet more words (like *sky, law, window*) to the language. Whatever the dialect variations in the speech of the original Anglo-Saxon settlers, the Danish occupation ensured the survival of major speech differences across the land, many of which remain clearly perceptible today. The Danes in their turn embraced Christianity, and the country moved steadily towards political unity.

In 1066 A.D., in a bizarre eddy on the fringe of the still-spreading tide of Indo-European speakers, a group that had earlier moved from Scandinavia into northern France, adopting the language of their new country but retaining the appellation of Norsemen or *Normans*, crossed the English Channel to rule, and later mingle with, the resident population of Anglo-Saxon and Danish descent. It is hard to overestimate the long-term impact of this development both on the language of the country and also therefore on the inhabitants' capacity for thought and action. The language of the Normans arrived more gradually than they did: Edward the Confessor and his court had spoken the language, and in many ways Normandy began to achieve cultural dominance before acquiring political and administrative control. But it took at least a couple of centuries before Norman French finally and fully combined with Anglo-Saxon or Old English to produce Middle English, and English men and women, fully conscious of their national identity, could exploit the wide range of distinctions their large vocabulary offered them – distinguishing with great delicacy and efficiency, for example, between the animals they fed (*sheep, bull, calf, pig, deer*) and the animals they ate (*mutton, beef, veal, pork, venison*).

Meanwhile in the mid-twelfth century further French influence of a rather different sort arrived in the person of Queen Eleanor of Aquitaine, just divorced from Louis VII of France, to marry Henry II of England. In Eleanor's train came the learning, literature and language of the high French Middle Ages as well as political and trade links with the duchy of Aquitaine. English vocabulary continued to absorb French words, this time from 'mainstream' French rather than its Norman variant, adding words like *wage, warranty* and *ward, chattel* and *chase* to *gage, guarantee,* and *guard, cattle* and *catch,* and thus increasing still further the capacity of the language to distinguish and classify experience.

Not until the late fourteenth century did Middle English achieve universal currency in England and French retire to the status of a school subject. Richard II was the first English king to have English as his first language, and at his court flourished the towering figure (metaphorically speaking: he describes himself as short and fat) of Geoffrey Chaucer (c. 1340-1400), whose vernacular poetry shaped the language and the nation as that of no other writer except perhaps Shakespeare has done. The statute requiring the use of English in law-suits – a crucial test of a language's status – passed into law in 1362. Lawyers, a conservative breed concerned to preserve the mystery of their calling, resisted this, and a kind of dog or bastard law-French survived for several centuries; the intriguing court-report to the effect that "le prisonier jecta un brick-bat à le dit juge, que narrowly mist" comes from the seventeenth.

During the century after Chaucer's death spoken English underwent some very rapid and violent changes in a process known as the Great Vowel Shift. Chaucer pronounced his English, the South-east Midland dialect, with vowel values very like those of modern French. We know, from the evidence of rhyme, of transliteration from other languages and indeed of the basically phonetic spelling systems used by scribes in those dictionary-free times, that he pronounced *white* somewhat as we pronounce *wheat,* and that he said *knight* with a similar vowel sound while pronouncing the initial *k* and giving the *gh* something of the guttural force of the *ch* in Scottish *loch:* without using phonetic symbols we would have to write something like *k'neecht.* Two centuries later, by Shakespeare's time, both words would have been pronounced in a way that we would at least recognise today even though minor changes have continued. Changes similar in general outline, though different in a multitude of details, took place at the same time in the other dialects of English that its chequered history had generated. Indeed, the dialects themselves borrowed from each other to supplement deficiencies in their range of utterance: southern dialects adopted northern third-person plural pronouns *they, them* and *their* in place of *hey, hem* and *hire,* and imported from the same source the valuable initial **s** on *she*. How on earth did they manage before?[1]

William Caxton (c. 1421-91), who introduced the printing-press into England and whose life spans the most intense period of the Great Vowel Shift, bears witness to the speed of the change and discusses some of the problems of translating Virgil's *Aeneid* into an English of such fluid linguistic values (Caxton's compositor largely interchanges the roles we normally assign to the letters **v** and **u**):

> And whan I had aduised me in this sayd boke, I delybered and concluded to translate it in-to englysshe, And forthwyth toke a penne & ynke, and wrote a leef or tweyne whyche I ouersawe agayn to corecte it. And whan I saw the fayr & straunge termes therin I doubted that it sholde not please some gentylmen whiche late blamed me, sayeng that in my translacyons I had ouer curyous termes whiche coude not be vnderstande of comyn peple, and desired me to vse olde and homely termes in my translacyons. and fayn wolde I satysfye euery man, and so to doo, toke an olde boke and redde therin, and certaynly the englysshe was so rude and brood that I coude not wele vnderstande it. And also my lorde abbot of westmynster ded do shewe to me late, certayn euydences [documents] wryton in olde englysshe, for to reduce it in-to our englysshe now vsid. And certaynly it was wreton in suche wyse that it was more lyke to dutche [German] than englysshe; I coude not reduce ne brynge it to be vnderstonden. And certaynly our langage now vsed varyeth ferre from that whiche was vsed and spoken when I was borne.
> For we englysshe men ben borne vnder the domynacyon of the mone, whiche is neuer stedfaste but euer wauerynge, wexynge one season and waneth & dyscreaseth another season.[2] And that comyn englysshe that is spoken in one shyre varyeth from a nother. In so moche that in my dayes happened that certayn marchauntes were in a shippe in tamyse [the river Thames] for to haue sayled ouer the see into zelande; and for lacke of wynde, they taryed atte forlond, and wente to lande for to refreshe them;
> And one of theym named sheffelde, a mercer, cam in-to an hows [inn] and axed for mete; and specyally he axyd after eggys; And the goode wyf answerde, that she coude speke no frenshe. And the marchaunt was angry, for he also coude speke no frenshe, but wolde haue hadde egges, and she vnderstod hym not. And thenne at laste a nother sayd that he wolde haue eyren; then the good wyf sayd that she vnderstod hym wel. Loo, what sholde a man in thyse dayes now wryte, egges or eyren . . .[3]

Although Caxton illustrates his predicament with an example of dialect differences he is struggling, in fact, with the early effects of the enormous influx of *borrowings* that was to pour into English for the next couple of hundred years. Communications within Europe were improving, and Europe was becoming aware of a wider world opening up with all the prospects it offered for exploration, empire-building and enrichment. As the wonders of the world were reported back to Britain, so were the words: the vocabularies of Greek and Latin were ransacked for terms with which to handle the new scientific and technological speculation; Spanish provided terms for exploration and for the developing technology of war such as *grenade, duel* and *barricade* (the enemy always does, witness *blitz*); Italian contributed a whole range of musical and artistic terms like *opera, piano, chiaroscuro,* and so on; and French lent a multitude of terms with particular emphasis on food, fashion and diplomacy (*cuisine, biscuit, mode, diplomacy* itself, and a host of others). These terms in general became known as *oversea language.* Those which served scholarship in particular were called *inkhorn terms.* Some of these, like *adiuvation, adminiculation* and *obtestation,* flourished for a while and then disappeared; others like *education* and *inclination* installed themselves permanently.

English, having thus got into the habit of borrowing, continued to practise it during the establishment of the British Empire in the eighteenth and nineteenth centuries, acquiring words not only from the languages of the newly colonized areas but also from those of European competitors for overseas possessions. Thus *siesta, coffee, tobacco, verandah, bungalow, jamboree, palaver* and hundreds of other words entered the language. The process continues, most vigorously perhaps in American English in response to the multiplicity of different language-groups represented within the U.S.A. as well as to that country's vigorous, if not always felicitous, participation in international affairs. Wars in particular shake up language just as they disrupt and discompose everything else in society: foreign terms are borrowed in wartime not by a literate minority which acknowledges their alien status but by ordinary people who need them for communcation and therefore absorb them fully into their demotic. Thus the French card game of *vingt-et-un* (twenty-one) entered English as *pontoon,*while the cry for help *m'aidez* became internationalised as *Mayday.* And international contact of any sort can generate odd exchanges, as bilingual signs on some of the cross-Channel steamers operating between Britain and France can testify:

> **The Buffet will be open at 11 o'clock**
> **Le Snack-bar sera ouvert à 11 heures**

Besides modifying its sound and acquiring the largest vocabulary any language has ever possessed, English has changed over the centuries in a variety of other ways. Old English, in common with German and with Indo-European languages in general, was a 'synthetic' language, indicating the contribution of words to their contexts by altering or *inflecting* 'bound forms' like suffixes. Thus *amo* in Latin means 'I love', *amant* means 'they love', *amavimus* means 'we have loved' and so on. Over the past thousand years English, unlike German but like French and some of the Latin-derived languages of modern Europe, has largely moved from *synthesis* to *analysis*, indicating an increasing number of word-relationships by means of additional terms (like *I, they, we* and *have* in the forms of the verb *love* quoted above). A few inflected suffixes survive, like the **-s** that indicates either plural number (except in a few cases like *children*) or the third person singular of the verb (*she walks*), and the **'s** (or **s'**) that indicates possession. Few as these are, they still generate confusion; some glossy publicity delivered to my mailbox yesterday from a well known grocery chain proclaimed not only *"This week's Kiwi Magic Plus Buys"* but also, by an unfortunate analogy, *"3 Week's of Kiwi Magic Prices"*.

This move to analysis has had profound results. In a synthetic language grammatical meaning does not depend on word-order: *puer amat puellam* and *puellam amat puer* both mean 'the boy loves the girl'. The difference in order generates differences in emphasis; we might translate the second 'it is the girl the boy loves'. In an analytic language word-order becomes crucial to meaning: *the boy loves the girl* is not at all the same as *the girl loves the boy*. (If it were, we would have to rewrite most of the history of the human race, and the whole of literature.)

Grammar and word-order therefore reflect the shift from synthesis to analysis, and the entire change has substantially modified the language's mimetic qualities.[4] Synthetic languages, as their name suggests, seem more ready to synthesize experience rather than merely analyse what is already there. Analytic languages on the other hand, limited in the word-order they can choose, probably imply a greater degree of pre-existent reality. Their speakers will certainly feel more bound by things like time and causality, a dependence that Lewis Carroll implicitly criticizes when he takes Alice through the looking-glass and makes all sorts of things happen 'back to front'. An analytic language will therefore encourage scientific speculation and the philosophical *realism* we discussed in Chaper 1 – which may account for the *nominalist* backlash today.

But Ernest Fenollosa's assertion that 'thought is successive . . . because the operations of nature are successive' may owe more to the operations of language than to those of nature herself. Indeed, his own analysis of the Chinese ideograms like the one for *rise* ('the sun is above the horizon, but beyond that the single upright line is like the growing trunk-line of the tree sign.') demonstrates the simultaneity of much of our experience.[5] We say "the boy kicks the ball" because we think that is the order in which it really happens. But the sentence describes one single unified act; we put *the boy* first because, language being linear, we have to start somewhere, and he seems to take the initiative – or if he doesn't, our word-order has few facilities for telling us so. An ancient Roman, on the other hand, voicing the same event, could have put the four words (*pede pilam percutit puer*) in whatever order best suited the speaker's exact perception of the event. The perception, that is to say, can more readily take priority over the event in a synthetic language.

Who indeed knows what is going on until language arrives to endow it with a local habitation and a name? The praetor Marcus Pomponius, announcing Rome's defeat by Hannibal in the battle of Lake Trasimene in 217 B.C., could have uttered the four words of his announcement to the anxious populace – *pugna magna victi sumus* – in any order; his choice not only reproduced the presumed general order of events but also kept his hearers in the longest possible suspense: our analytical language restricts us either to losing the suspense: 'we have been defeated in a big battle,' or to clumsy longwindedness: 'there's been a battle – a big one – someone's come out loser – us'.[6] A colleague of mine has described Pomponius's utterance as 'the ultimate press-release'.

We should not therefore conclude that the shift from synthesis to analysis represents unqualified improvement, some kind of upward linguistic evolution. Nevertheless an analytic language, with its vastly increased vocabulary, can distinguish very fine shades of meaning: we can translate Latin *amo* as *I love, I am loving* or *I do love*, each of which contributes something different and unique to our range of utterance and therefore of experience.

Just as examining another language alerts us to the potential and limitations of our own, so some idea of the history of English should remind us of the temporary and contingent nature of what our language allows us to say at any one moment. The other major area of change in English, semantic shift, reinforces this. Word-meanings change constantly, as we saw in our discussion of metaphor in Chapter 2. As shadowy new experiences grope for words to embody them, we can of course invent new ones: acronyms like UNESCO and AIDS (often now written Aids) frequently do the job; a few combination terms have stuck, like *smog, motel* and Lewis Carroll's *chortle*. Surprisingly few terms have been invented from scratch: the seventeenth century Dutch chemist J. B. Van Helmont concocted the word *gas* for what he believed to be an ultra-rarified condition of water but confessed that he had probably based the word in the Greek word for *chaos* (he also coined *blas*, which has not survived). As readers of Chapter 1 will not be surprised to find, only when the word existed could the *thing* as we now know it (hydrogen, carbon dioxide and so on) achieve full existence in people's minds.

Usually, of course, we voice new experiences by means of words ready to hand, bringing into operation some species of metaphor. We bend the word to fit the thing, and put new wine in old bottles – as in the case of the computer terminology we examined in Chapter 2; but often we fail to realise that to some extent the thing bends to fit the word: we give a dog a bad name and hang it, or, contrariwise, call gangs *motorcycle clubs* and hope for behaviour appropriate to that title. The homosexual community pre-empted the word *gay* presumably as an encouragement to themselves as much as a sign to the rest of the world. All this results, of course, in the kind of ambiguity we examined in Chaper 5 and endorses the subjectivity we acknowledged as inevitable in Chapter 6.

This semantic radiation occurs constantly. *Gas* provides us with a nice example: whatever its exact scientific definition (if one exists), the word has spread amoebically to absorb, among other things, flatulence, a particularly filthy form of warfare, petrol, vapid talk and whatever referent underlies the word in the phrase *all gas and gaiters*. Meanings, however, not only absorb and reproduce like amoebas but bloom, wither, and die like roses in summer: the word *nice* I used just now has enjoyed one of the most varied range of meanings imaginable since its introduction into English seven hundred years ago in the sense of 'stupid, foolish' (from Latin *nescius*, 'ignorant'). Its meanderings, too complex to trace in detail here, passed from *stupid* through some such sequence as *naive, innocent, harmless, unspoilt, pure, delicate, precious, refined, expensive* and *desirable*, to end with today's general and unspecific term of approval – except in certain precise contexts like *a nice distinction*, which preserves the *delicate* sense, in fossil form as it were. Context indeed proves a very powerful preservative, and medicine a very potent context: *small* in its Middle English sense of 'slender' survives in *the small intestine*, while the aqueous and vitreous *humours* of the eye enshrine a physical sense of the word (from Latin *humidus*, 'moist') that otherwise gave way to psychological expressions of temper and comedy (*in an ill humour, a sense of humour*) well before the end of the seventeenth century.

The series of historical accidents (or crimes) that foisted English upon the world as its chief vehicle for international communication did not of course pause to consider the language's suitability for this role. As it turned out, and in spite of the irregularities and absurdities of English, the world could have done much worse. Its readiness to absorb new vocabulary has meant that most new speakers could find something of their own language in it – even if only words previously borrowed by that language from English. Its relative lack of inflected word-endings, and its subject/verb/object grammatical order, mean that new speakers can make shift at least to survive in it with comparatively little experience. Besides the estimated 330 million people who speak it as their first language, therefore, about the same number again speak it as a second language: a railway official coming from North India to investigate problems in the south communicates in English, as does air-traffic control at Madrid airport to the Spanish pilot of a Spanish airliner coming in to land. The teaching of English as a second language has become very big international business indeed.

This universality has produced two apparently incompatible results. For official communication of the sort needed by airlines, business people and diplomats a limited, homogenous English has developed, narrow in vocabulary and generally based on the written conventions of the South-east Midland dialect whose rise we chronicled in Chapter 4. It demands, and as often as not gets, the 'mid-Atlantic' pronunciation that has emerged since the Second World War as the result of intense mass media exchanges between the major English-speaking population groups. But where English has taken root as a local language, as it continues to do in various parts of the world, it has rapidly acquired local characteristics and dialect features that have quickly rendered it largely unintelligible to other English speakers. The various kinds of Pidgin English that developed in Africa and all over the New World, sometimes settling into fully established Creole dialects, may serve as the most colourful example.

A survey of the history of the English language thus reinforces several of the issues that have emerged in previous chapters of this book. The speed with which the language changes, and the variety of shapes it takes at different times and in different places, must further invalidate any claims it may make to any real objectivity. Clearly its mimetic or 'poetic' capacities will vary with its vocabulary, with its structure and with its readiness to handle and acknowledge metaphor. Perhaps the openness of sixteenth and early seventeenth century speakers to new words and ideas and therefore to metaphor accounts for the astonishing vigour of the language during that period, making possible the plays of Shakespeare and enabling a committee of Anglican theologians to produce, in the King James version of the Bible, their own timeless masterpiece. The same thing has happened at other times and in other places too:

All art is collaboration; and there is little doubt that in the happy ages of literature, striking and beautiful phrases were as ready to the story-teller's or the play-wright's hand, as the rich cloaks and dresses of his time. It is probable that when the Elizabethan dramatist took his ink-horn and sat down to his work he used many phrases that he had just heard, as he sat at dinner, from his mother or his children. In Ireland, those of us who know the people have the same privilege. When I was writing *The Shadow of the Glen*, some years ago, I got more aid than any learning could have given me from a chink in the floor of the old Wicklow house where I was staying, that let me hear what was being said by the servant girls in the kitchen. This matter, I think, is of importance, for in countries where the imagination of the people, and the language they use, is rich and living, it is possible for a writer to be rich and copious in his words, and at the same time to give the reality, which is the root of all poetry, in a comprehensive and natural form. . . . In a good play every speech should be as fully flavoured as a nut or apple, and such speeches cannot be written by anyone who works among people who have shut their lips on poetry. In Ireland, for a few years more, we have a popular imagination that is fiery, and magnificent, and tender: so that those of us who wish to write start with a chance that is not given to writers in places where the spring-time of the local life has been forgotten, and the harvest is a memory only, and the straw has been turned into bricks[7]

For writers, the moral of a study of the history of language would seem to be *Make sure you are born at the right time and in the right place.* Failing that, *Do your best, by the way you use language, to make it so.*

Notes

1 By writing *heo*, or *ho*, or by guessing.
2 Medieval science divided the Earth into seven zones, each under the influence of one of the seven planets of the Ptolomaic system (the Moon, Mercury, Venus, the Sun, Mars, Jupiter and Saturn). England was in the Lunar zone, which was perhaps why, when Hamlet was diagnosed as mad, King Claudius sent him there – where he would appear no different from anyone else.
3 Caxton pp.1-3
4 see Chapter 1
5 Fenollosa p.33
6 Livy, *History of Rome* XXII, 7
7 Synge pp.183-5

10

THE TEACHING OF WRITING

The lyf so short, the craft so long to lerne
Chaucer

You cannot teach writing – not, at least, writing in the sense in which this book uses the word. You can of course teach calligraphy to a reasonably apt pupil, and teachers and parents regularly perform wonders in teaching learners and children to shape their letters and string them together into words. But writing as we have discussed it in this book, the kind that creates communicatively and communicates creatively, remains at least as much an art as a craft. No two writing tasks ever pose quite the same problems, so that no tried solution ever works twice. If "every attempt is a wholly new start, and a different kind of failure" then formal instruction can do little to help.

Handbooks nevertheless proliferate, many of them crafted with care, scholarship and insight. Scrutiny reveals a few of them to be themselves atrociously written, which should warn potential users to take no notice at all of anything they purport to teach. Most, however, represent the labours and experience of capable teachers who want to get on permanent record techniques that they have found to work in the classroom. But even the best has a strangely daunting effect on the would-be learner: writing is a complicated business, susceptible of scholarly analysis into an almost endless catalogue of parts and processes, and it all looks so long, with so much to remember – about paragraph development and parallel construction, pre-writing strategies and prepositional phrases, footnotes, focusing statements and stylistic flow, and so on and so on. "Do I have to learn all this," asks the student, "before I can start writing?"

Of course not. The best of such handbooks take the reader/writer through a carefully graded course, concentrating perhaps upon the different stages of the writing process or upon different types and genres of writing, judiciously rationing the advice to suit the task in hand so that it never overwhelms the recipient. Illustrations often lighten the tone and relieve the intensity, and quotations illuminate the salient points. In the hands of a capable teacher a handbook of this kind can prove helpful and stimulating, though that teacher will almost certainly adapt and select, while the plethora of handbooks itself further suggests the existence of as many effective methods as effective teachers while reminding us that every attempt to produce a satisfactory handbook on writing is, in its own way, also a different kind of failure.

All of which in turn implies the importance of the teacher, not so much in the role of instructor as in that of facilitator or mediator, and returns us to the point with which we begin this chapter. You cannot teach writing: but you can set up an environment in which your students will want to teach themselves (or even, as we shall see in a minute) each other. You can, with skill, experience and luck, stimulate learner-writers to discover, in practice (and often indeed without being able fully to articulate them) many of the precepts and principles which the handbooks spell out at such forbidding length. As a teacher, you possess the very great advantage over a handbook of being a person. Whatever it may claim to the contrary, the book, by its very existence, must convey to its reader the view of writing as a solitary, one-ended pastime to be pursued, initially at least, for purposes of self-gratification in the silence and isolation of the study. A handbook can provide no audience, and can therefore equip the writing with very little real purpose. A teacher of good will, even though far less fully versed than the writer of the handbook in the theoretical minutiae of the writing process, can operate a thousand times better by getting the learner interested, enthusiastic and committed to the task at hand. You can't make the horse drink, but you can take steps to make it thirsty.

You can do this in a variety of ways. As we saw in Chapter 7, the urge to write seems to spring from some inexplicable or even irrational drive to do so – what Kipling called his *daemon* – or from the need to communicate something to some kind of audience. These two may in the end be the same thing, or at least different aspects of the same thing. The *daemon* of course remains unaccountable; he is a metaphor, and if we did not find his tenor hard to grasp we would not have to resort to this and all the other creaking vehicles by which we seek to convey it. In any case he either is, or is not, and we can do little about it either way.

But most of us possess a decent amount of self-esteem, and enjoy the admiration of an audience. A surprising number of us also have something of value to say to our fellow mortals, though that message, when we come to write it down, may emerge surprisingly different from what we imagined it to be in the first place; and indeed our readers may continue to find what we write valuable and interesting for reasons we never intended or even dreamed of. That too is unaccountable, and universal, and probably something to do with the *daemon*. But it does remind us that the overwhelming bulk of the writing produced in this world is intended for some kind of publication, the last of the six stages of the writing process we listed in Chapter 7, and indeed makes little or no sense without it.

To catch the *daemon*, therefore, a wise teacher uses a bait of publication – whether that means sending the finished product home after school, or pinning it up on the classroom wall, or printing it in the class or school magazine, or entering it for a competition, or mailing it to a newspaper or professional journal, or simply sharing it aloud with a small group on the spot. This strategy almost never fails; the rest follows in its train and becomes simply a matter for detailed tactics, important but unlikely to influence the overall outcome of the campaign. With publication in view, students will discuss their ideas more freely and less self-consciously than they might without it; they will draft with care and revise with the needs and quirks of their prospective audience in mind; they will even bother with the tedium of proof-reading, often undertaking the task for someone else partly out of kindness and partly out of curiosity. They will want to 'get it right' and will search any available handbook or pick the teacher's brains on matters of grammar, tone, meaning, impact and so on. In the course of time they will acquire expertise, discrimination, tact, and a realistic humility – some important components of a liberal education, in fact.

The only audience whom they should not habitually address is the teacher in person – for whom the bulk of writing in school and university has traditionally been produced. Students over the years have shown redoubtable patience, and sometimes noteworthy cunning, in writing for an audience which they must presume will know far more than they themselves about most of the topics set, and which will almost certainly be less interested in what they have to say than in how they say it. Northrop Frye touches on this absurd and indeed forbidding arrangement when he describes the academic thesis as "a document which is, practically by definition, something that nobody particularly wants either to write or to read".[1] Even in such barren surroundings the *daemon* sometimes manifests itself, though often half suffocated by lack of interest or in forlornly domesticated and regulated guise. Later, perhaps, when the students have become accustomed to writing for audiences that really want to read what they have to say, a teacher can move back in, deliberately, consciously, and in all due humility, as audience – at the risk of encountering some fairly painful home truths through the agency of the style and tone the students evidently consider appropriate.

In this imperfect world teachers cannot, unfortunately, always find a live audience for their students to address. But it is always possible to pretend, and students usually possess enough patience and good humour to join in the game, sometimes even with enthusiasm. Since we have it on good authority that their *whole vocation* is *endless imitation* such an activity would not seem at all out of harmony with the role of language and of writing as we examined it in Chapter 1. As usual, the dividing line between truth and fiction remains, in daily experience, blurred.

To add colour and variety to the game, teachers may find it useful to exploit the four variables which we identified in our exploration of *meaning* in Chapter 3, gathering them under the acronym **RAFT.**

The acronym RAFT is a useful device for exploring the range of writing possibilities. R is role, A is audience, F is format, and T is topic. Let's say we have chosen 'Corporal Punishment' as the topic for a writing assignment. Here are some possibilities for combining R, A and F with T:

Role	Audience	Format	Topic
Parent	friend	telegram	Corporal punishment
Journalist	headmaster	letter	
Cane	editor of maga-zine or newspaper	pamphlet	
Politician	Minister of Education	article	
Student	other canes	memo	
Deputy Principal	school assembly	speech	

Once I have assembled the various possibilities for R, A, and F to match T, I then link up the combinations I want for a particular writing assignment. If I wanted to teach conciseness in expression, I would match up Deputy Principal (R) with Minister of Education (A) and telegram (F). If I wanted to teach point-of-view (from an eccentric angle and with humour), I would match up Cane (R) with Other Canes (A) and speech (F). With R, A, and F elements assembled, I would then compose a carefully worded assignment-task to provide the necessary focus; 'As Deputy Principal of a Co-ed School, write a telegram to the Minister of Education supporting his views on corporal punishment'; or 'As the chief executing cane, write a speech to other canes for the purpose of boosting their waning morale'. Preliminary discussion of the respective formats (telegram, speech) would probably be necessary.[2]

Such a technique clearly provides a good method of alerting students to the wide range of points of view available on any topic and indeed to the whole question of subjectivity we discussed in Chapter 6. It is hard to think of a better way to introduce young people to the kaleidoscopic world awaiting them outside their immediate experience, and possibly to demonstrate the power of the oblique and ironic for making a case or persuading an audience.

Many teachers in recent years have also turned to the technique known as **peer-editing**, whereby students, in groups or (more usually) pairs, scrutinize and comment on each other's writing. This technique achieves several good results of several different kinds. Students usually enjoy and gain reassurance from looking at each other's work. By removing the total emphasis from the final act of marking, the technique removes quite a burden from the back of a busy English teacher whose marking load often outweighs that of colleagues in other disciplines. It also, paradoxically, provides student writers with a potential audience of far greater influence than the teacher usually wields. Students automatically expect their teacher to be fastidious about a variety of academic (in the worst sense) issues when marking an assignment. It is normal to get your assignment back covered with a rash of red marks of which you take little or no notice; you simply find out how your mark compares with those of your friends before consigning the whole thing to the oblivion of desk or folder. If, on the other hand, a class-mate looks at your writing while you are still doing it and complains that a particular passage does not make sense or makes different sense from what you intended, then you will pay rather more attention and take steps to rectify things. You may well ask the teacher for help in doing so. And the commitment that this generates may even persuade you to bother more than before about what the teacher thinks of your work when you have finished it.

Peer-editing has its drawbacks too, of course. Students initially find it intimidating both to scrutinize someone else's writing and have theirs scrutinized in turn. "Writing", some of my students occasionally protest (unconsciously voicing a strong Romantic tradition) "is such a private activity". If I have time, I give them a précis of Chapter 8 of this book by way of reply, and in any case a little experience of peer-editing not only lays its spectres but convincingly demonstrates the enormous resources it offers.

A fellow student's scrutiny will admittedly pick up by no means all the mistakes in a piece of writing, and some teachers feel concern at the number of errors thus becoming reinforced by practice. Students may sometimes criticize each other too harshly, and a writer's tentatively budding self-esteem get trampled underfoot. More frequently the opposite happens when an undiscriminating peer-editor, too kind or too shy or too indolent to bother, rhapsodizes about very indifferent stuff and sends the writer away with self-esteem inflated to a state of unhealthy and totally unjustified hypertrophy.

With careful planning, teachers can avoid most of these drawbacks. Students working in pairs and editing each other's work soon learn, in the interests of survival and peaceful co-existence, to discipline their approach and provide each other with a fair deal. Peer-editors lacking in experience or confidence will work best if given very precise jobs to do and very specific questions to answer. It should be a matter of courtesy not to scribble all over one's partner's script unless invited to, so editors do best to make marks only down one of the margins: usually a cross against anything that seems wrong, a tick against anything that seems particularly effective, and a question-mark against anything that puzzles them will provide plenty of material for discussion when writer and editor finally confer about the latter's findings (usually of course each is editing the other's, so they have to confer twice, their only problem being which script to start with). An injunction from the teacher to be sure to use both crosses and ticks while limiting both to within a specified number will usually restrain the hostile editor and discipline the uncritical one. And while some errors may indeed continue to slip through, that seems a small price to pay for the vastly increased responsibility that students begin to feel for their writing, and the tremendous upsurge in their awareness of what it is all about that usually accompanies a growing experience of peer-editing. Before long they will be ashamed of *any* errors that survive in their work, and go to extraordinary lengths to eradicate them.

Peer-editing can, in my experience, profitably take place even between students of widely differing abilities. A fluent and advanced writer often benefits from the scrutiny of a reader of slow understanding, learning clarity and control from the experience; while a great deal of valuable informal tuition takes place in the reverse direction, with the 'tutor' probably learning quite a lot by having to articulate it.

Having thus, in one way or another, survived the scrutiny of another person, students will then much more readily discuss their work in a group, exploring – often with surprising detachment and objectivity – the craft of the writing process and the various techniques (and sometimes tricks) with which its practitioners may encompass it. The teacher may well have a specific point to make as a consequence of the editing session, in which case the students will, with any luck, see it without too much prompting. The teacher will very likely have set up the whole exercise in order to teach a particular aspect of writing, and should be thankful if all goes according to plan while prepared to make some quick adjustments if it doesn't. But such sessions rarely fail to throw up something of value for exploitation by an alert and flexible teacher. In my experience the teacher often learns as much as the students: these moments of shared pursuit of the truth constitute one of the great rewards of the teaching profession.

Such moments sometimes occur by chance. More frequently they materialize as the reward of long and careful planning. Good teachers of writing have always analysed not only the writing process but also the needs, backgrounds and abilities of the students, matching each to the other in a way that again no handbook can emulate. As long ago as 1934 Ezra Pound was advocating peer-editing while disclaiming any originality for the idea:

Most human perceptions date from a long time ago, or are derivable from perceptions that gifted men have had long before we were born. The race discovers, and rediscovers.

TESTS AND COMPOSITION EXERCISES

I

1 Let the pupils exchange composition papers and see how many and what useless words have been used – how many words that convey nothing new.
2 How many words that obscure the meaning.
3 How many words out of their usual place, and whether this alteration makes the statement in any way more interesting or more energetic.
4 Whether a sentence is ambiguous; whether it really means more than one thing or more than the writer intended; whether it can be so read as to mean something different.
5 Whether there is something clear on paper, but ambiguous if spoken aloud.

II

It is said that Flaubert taught De Maupassant to write. When De Maupassant returned from a walk Flaubert would ask him to describe someone, say a concierge whom they would both pass in their next walk, and to describe the person so that Flaubert would recognize, say, the concierge and not mistake her for some other concierge and not the one De Maupassant had described.

SECOND SET

1 Let the pupil write the description of a tree.
2 Of a tree without mentioning the name of the tree (larch, pine, etc.) so that the reader will not mistake it for the description of some other kind of tree.
3 Try some object in the class-room.
4 Describe the light and shadow on the school-room clock or some other object.
5 If it can be done without breach of the peace, the pupil could write descriptions of some other pupil. The author suggests that the pupil should not describe the instructor, otherwise the description might become a vehicle of emotion, and subject to more complicated rules of composition than the class is yet ready to cope with.

In all these descriptions the test would be accuracy and vividness, the pupil receiving the other's paper would be the gauge. He would recognize or not recognize the object or person described . . .

FURTHER TESTS

1 Let the pupils in exchanging themes judge whether the theme before them really says anything.
2 Let them judge whether it tells them anything or 'makes them see anything' they hadn't noticed before, especially in regard to some familiar scene or object.
3 Variant: whether the writer really had to KNOW something about the subject or scene before being able to write the page under consideration.[3]

Techniques such as peer-editing not only have the authority of Ezra Pound and the sanction of the common sense of many experienced teachers of writing, but an increasing amount of research is confirming their effectiveness in improving the performance of student-writers in work done for other subjects as well as in their 'English' assignments.[4]

The chemistry of the teaching of writing remains mysterious, however: many different methods have achieved spectacular ends in the long history of education:

> Behind *Paradise Lost*, behind *Hamlet*, behind *The Faerie Queene*, lay years of daily practice in translating Latin into English, English into Latin, endless themes written and corrected and rewritten, endless copying and imitation of the Classical writers, endless working and reworking of long lists of rhetorical devices with immense Greek names. Discipline of this kind is apparently impossible in the modern school, where teachers are not only overworked but subjected to anti-literary pressures. They are encouraged, sometimes compelled, to substitute various kinds of slick verbal trash for

literature; they are bedevilled with audiovisual and other aids to distraction; their curricula are prescribed by a civil service which in its turn responds to pressure from superstitious or prurient voters. In the verbal arts, the student of eighteen is about where he should be at fourteen, apart from what he does on his own with the help of a sympathetic teacher or librarian. To say this is not to reflect on the schools, but on the social conditions that cripple them.[5]

Whatever the differences, however, between our systems for teaching writing and those which produced Milton, Shakespeare and Spenser, two principles survive unaltered: the best way to learn to write is to write, and the teacher remains an essential catalyst in the whole reaction. To this we might add a third principle: teachers of writing do the job better if they themselves habitually write. A busy teaching life usually makes this a hard principle to put into practice, but increasing numbers of teachers are taking advantage of the 'Writing Projects' coming into existence round the English-speaking world, often supported by universities or by governmental or local Departments of Education. Many a teaching career has been rejuvenated by participation in one of these Projects. The **RAFT** exercise quoted earlier in this chapter resulted from one organized annually by my own university.

Most teachers, furthermore, remain in general agreement that instruction in formal grammar serves as a most inefficient way of teaching people to write. Sir Philip Sidney certainly thought so:

> Another will say, it [the English language] wanteth Grammer. Nay truly it hath that praise that it wants not Grammer; for Grammer it might have, but it needs it not, being so easie in it selfe, and so voyde of those combersome differences of *Cases, Genders, Moods, & Tenses,* which I thinke was a peece of the Tower of *Babilons* curse, that a man should be put to schoole to learn his mother tongue. But for the uttering sweetly and properly the conceit of the minde, which is the end of speech, that hath it equally with any other tongue in the world.[6]

A modern grammarian explores the case further:

> Grammar is notoriously the most widely and deeply hated of all studies, at least in English-speaking countries. Several reasons, each containing at least some truth, have been advanced to explain this fact. One is that the kind of grammar that has been traditionally taught in our schools is based on Latin, and fits English so loosely that considerable parts of it can be understood only as an act of faith, with a distinct element of mysticism. Another is that the subject is often taught not as a body of information but as a system of morals,

toward which we often have a split reaction. While one side of our minds tells us that we ought to obey the rules because they must somehow be right, the other tells us that if we do we'll lose many of our friends, and feel like prigs in the process. And finally there is the widespread suspicion that the whole subject is unnecessary – an imposition foisted on us by schoolteachers and their ilk. "Why," asks young Tommy, "have any parts of speech at all? What are they good for? Why don't they just let us talk sense?"[7]

We should be careful not to legislate, however, even about this. There seems no limit to what a capable teacher can achieve, with even the most intractable of materials. Of his experiences after entering the bottom form of Harrow School in 1886 Winston Churchill writes:

> I continued in this unpretentious situation for nearly a year. However, by being so long in the lowest form I gained an immense advantage over the cleverer boys. They all went on to learn Latin and Greek and splendid things like that. But I was taught English. We were considered such dunces that we could learn only English. Mr Somervell – a most delightful man, to whom my debt is great – was charged with the duty of teaching the stupidest boys the most disregarded thing – namely, to write mere English. He knew how to do it. He taught it as no one else has ever taught it. Not only did we learn English parsing thoroughly, but we also practised continually English analysis. Mr Somervell had a system of his own. He took a fairly long sentence and broke it up into its components by means of black, red, blue and green inks. Subject, verb, object: Relative Clauses, Conditional Clauses, Conjunctive and Disjunctive Clauses! Each had its colour and its bracket. It was a kind of drill. We did it almost daily. As I remained in the Third Form (β) three times as long as anyone else, I had three times as much of it. I learned it thoroughly. Thus I got into my bones the essential structure of the ordinary British sentence – which is a noble thing. And when in after years my schoolfellows who had won prizes and distinction for writing such beautiful Latin poetry and pithy Greek epigrams had to come down again to common English, to earn their living or make their way, I did not feel myself at any disadvantage. Naturally I am biased in favour of boys learning English. I would make them all learn English: and then I would let the clever ones learn Latin as an honour, and Greek as a treat. But the only thing I would whip them for is not knowing English. I would whip them hard for that.[8]

If Northrop Frye is right in speaking of "the summer of 1940 when the free world had practically nothing but Churchill's prose style left to fight with",[9] planet Earth in the second half of the twentieth century owes a debt of some magnitude to Mr Somervell. Few activities emerge as more important than the teaching of writing, and we must acknowledge those who do it well as very influential people indeed.

Notes

1 Frye p.10
2 O'Connor, Gerard. *RAFT*, in The Manawatu Writing Project 1986, Massey University, New Zealand.
3 Pound pp. 64-6
4 see for example Lamb, H: *Writing Performance in New Zealand Schools*, Department of Education, Wellington, 1987; McManus G and D. Kirby: 'Using Peer Group Instruction to Teach Writing' *English Journal* March 1988, 78-9; Pritchard R: 'Effects on Student Writing of Teacher Training in the National Writing Project Model' *Written Communication* 41, January 1987, 51-67.
5 Frye p.12
6 Sidney pp. 43-4
7 Myers pp. 255-6
8 Churchill pp. 24-5
9 Frye p.22

APPENDIX

Writing and Peer-editing Exercises

The following exercises put into practice some of the principles for the teaching of writing discussed in Chapter 10. Students should do the exercises in pairs, because editing someone else's work teaches some valuable lessons not otherwise readily available.

General Suggestions

The editing instructions for each exercise are divided into four stages. Writers and editors should make themselves familiar with all four before starting, and, if circumstances allow it, should confer and share their findings **after each stage**, proceeding to the next only when all emergent issues have been dealt with. In a school or university course, each exercise should occupy two or three class-periods, giving time for writers to redraft their work in the interim. The assignments suggested here are tailored to enable partners to work at a distance, through the mail if necessary.

Editors will need:
- three pens (**red, green,** and **blue** or **black**)
- a reasonably up to date **dictionary** (one published since 1960)
- an outline of English **grammar** such as David Crystal's *Rediscover Grammar* (see Suggestions for Further Reading in the Bibliography)
- plenty of **tact**. Remember that your editorial partner will be sensitive to criticism, so find fault kindly, and encourage as well as censure. Nevertheless, the best service you can render is to give a full and reasoned account of your honest reaction to your partner's work: it is, after all, what you will expect in return.

Exercise 1

WRITING:

Witnesses in some courts of law swear to tell 'the truth, the whole truth and nothing but the truth.' Write a letter of not more than 500 words to the editor of a newspaper or magazine whose readers might take an interest in such matters, giving your views on the capacity of language to achieve this.

Tell your editor the name and nature of the publication you are writing to. You may find Chapter 1 helpful in stimulating your ideas on this topic.

EDITING:

1. Begin by reading your partner's letter straight through, putting ? in the margin against any word or statement that does not seem totally and immediately clear to you, whatever the reason. Then **proof-read** the letter until it is 'print-ready', i.e. suitable for type-setting without further modification unless the writer so desires. To do this you need to check that the writer has observed the word–limit and all appropriate conventions of spelling, punctuation, layout and typography. Write X in **blue** or **black** in the margin against each obvious error, or any aspect of the writing that feels wrong, even though you may not be able to identify the fault. If you need to question or comment use a number (?1, ?2, X1, X2 etc.) and a footnote. Then check your own proofreading by reading the **last** sentence and working in reverse, sentence by sentence, to the start.

2. Underline in **red** the letter's **focusing statement** – the sentence (or clause or phrase) that encapsulates its thesis, gist or thrust. Then write, in **red** on a separate sheet, answers to the following questions:
    (a) How well does the focusing statement work?
        Is it accurate, or misleading in any way?
        Does it stimulate the reader to read on?
        How? Could it be improved? If so, how?
    (b) Is it in the best place, or would it be more effective earlier or later? Give reasons for your answer.
3. Underline in **green** two words or phrases that seem to you to 'tell the

truth' with particular success or effectiveness. Explain, in **green** on a separate sheet, why you have chosen them.

4. Add in **black** or **blue** any further comments you think may help the writer. How well, for example, does the letter suit the readership of its chosen publication? Is it paragraphed effectively and helpfully? Is it interesting? Is it persuasive? Give reasons for all the points you make.

Exercise 2

WRITING:

As Editor of the same publication, respond to a recent letter about the mimetic function of language (your Exercise 1) with an editorial of not more than 600 words assessing the part metaphor plays in conveying 'the truth'.

Chapter 2 discusses metaphor.

EDITING:

1. Read through your partner's editorial, identifying anything not fully clear by means of ? in the margin. Then proof-read it to a state of 'print-readiness', using the methods you used for Exercise 1. Test whether reading aloud reveals any further errors. Underline the focusing statement in **red**. Check that the editorial observes the 600 word limit.

2. Identify the editorial's introductory and concluding sections, inserting a **red** asterisk (*) in the text at the end of the introduction, and another at the start of the conclusion. On a separate sheet, in **red**, give your reasons for choosing these places, and comment on how the bit in between hangs together and develops. Add any suggestions for structural improvement that occur to you.

3. Underline in **green** two examples of effective metaphor (avoiding metaphors deliberately quoted as examples by the writer). Draw a **green** ring around a passage that might be improved by introducing or developing a metaphor, and append suggestions in **green** on a separate sheet.

4. Add in **blue** or **black** any further comments which you think might help the writer. Are any of the writer's metaphors, for example, too far-fetched, too obvious, or misleading in any way? Pay particular attention to the writer's use of the *passive voice,* and be alert for unnecessary repetition. Is there anything else distracting or annoying? Anything particularly effective? As always, give reasons.

Exercise 3

WRITING:

What makes a piece of English correct or incorrect? To demonstrate your answer to this question, write a short story about a piece of incorrect English and its consequences. The story should contain no more than 750 words, and be suitable for publication in a collection of short stories for children aged 10-12.

Chapter 4 discusses correctness. You may find it worthwhile to distinguish carefully between *written* and *spoken* language in thinking about the topic.

EDITING:

1. Read through as usual, and proof-read to 'print-readiness'. But remember that short stories may contain deliberate 'mistakes': not everyone, for example, speaks grammatically. If in doubt, use a footnote in the usual way. Check that the story is **punctuated** consistently, especially when anyone talks.

2. Identify the idea of correctness the story illustrates. Does it emerge clearly? Do you find it persuasive? How far is it an essential part of the story? Answer these questions in **blue** or **black** on a separate piece of paper, adding any comments and suggestions you think might help the writer.

3. From whose **point of view** is the story told (see Chapter 6)? Is the narrator a participant in the story or telling it from outside? How do you know, and what do you learn about the narrator as you read? Is there more than one point of view within the narrative? Underline in **green** one phrase, clause or sentence where the words convey someone's point of view (not necessarily the narrator's) with particular effectiveness. Explain in **green** why you chose that piece, adding any suggestions that occur to you for handling or exploiting point of view better. Does the story contain **irony** or deliberate **ambiguity** of any sort (see Chapter 5)? If so, underline in **red** an effective example of one or the other, appending your comments and suggestions in **red**.

4. Add in **black** or **blue** any further comments which you think might be of help to the writer. How well, for example, does the story suit its juvenile audience? Then trace your own reactions during your first reading of the story, and during subsequent readings if they differ. Give reasons for all your findings.

Exercise 4

WRITING:

Write the script for a five-minute talk, to be broadcast as part of an educational radio programme, under the title 'I mean what I say, but do I say what I mean?'

Chapter 3 discusses meaning.

EDITING:

1. Read through the script, then proof-read as meticulously as before, using all the techniques and resources you have now acquired. Check, as far as you can, that the script observes the five-minute time limit.

2. As before, underline in **red** the focusing statement, and indicate with **red** asterisks the junctions between the script's beginning, middle and end. Append explanatory or critical comments in **red**.

3. Underline in **green** two phrases, clauses or sentences where the writer has, in your opinion, generated the informal **tone** suitable to a radio talk without sacrificing brevity, clarity or accuracy. Draw a **green** ring round one passage where you see room for improvement – where something could be put more briefly without detriment to its meaning, or where clarity could be increased. Pay particular attention to the writer's use of the **passive voice** and be alert for unnecessary repetition. Append in **green** suggestions for improvement, with explanations.

4. Add in **blue** or **black** any further comments which you think might be of help to the writer. For example, what kind of personality (attractive or otherwise) seems to lurk behind the script? Has the talk modified your own views or feelings in any way? In what ways is the script particularly suitable for listening to rather than for reading silently? Any tongue-twisters? Anything distracting or annoying? Anything strikingly good?

Exercise 5

From the material quoted in this book, prepare an article for inclusion in a book on *Writers and Writing* intended for senior forms in secondary schools. Choose as your subject ONE of the following:

Alexander Pope; Jonathan Swift; Samuel Johnson; William Hazlitt; Oscar Wilde; Rudyard Kipling; Ernest Fenollosa; Winston Churchill; Ezra Pound; George Orwell; Northrop Frye; Irina Ratushinskaya.

To write the article:

(1) Write or type an accurate copy of a passage of reasonable length (at least 200 words) by your chosen writer.

(2) Discuss, in 800–1000 words, the qualities of its writing – its diction, point of view, tone, structure and anything else you find important to the way it establishes its meaning.

Write or type out your chosen passage attentively and early: you will learn a great deal while doing so. With your article, furnish your editor with editing instructions to suit your own needs, identifying any particular problems with which you need help.

EDITING:

Check the accuracy of the writer's copy, word by word. Note in the margin any corrections needed. Then respond as helpfully as you can to the writer's instructions, adding any points that strike you independently.

Exercise 6

WRITING:

Submit to your editor a recent piece of writing of your own (one of your earlier Exercises, perhaps – or indeed anything else) together with a commentary of 800–1000 words explaining its background and development and giving particular attention to the choices, great and small, you faced while writing it and the decisions you took about structure, diction, tone, point of view, meaning and so on – the 'inside story' of its development that you alone can tell. Your chosen piece must therefore be recent enough for you to be able to remember such things, of course.

Furnish your editor with appropriate instructions.

EDITING:

Respond to the writer's requests and instructions. Otherwise you are now on your own – but you may like to note the implications about yourself that emerge from the way the writer addresses you.

BIBLIOGRAPHY

(All works published in London unless otherwise stated)

Suggestions for further reading:

Auerbach, Erich. *Mimesis : the Representation of Reality in Western Literature.* Princeton N.J: Princeton U.P., 1953.
Crystal, David. *Rediscover Grammar.* Longman, 1988.
Dubrow, Heather. *Genre.* Methuen, 1982.
Hawkes, Trevor. *Metaphor.* Methuen, 1972.
Jackson, Howard. *Words and their Meaning.* Longman, 1988.
Muecke, D.C. *Irony and the Ironic.* Methuen, 1982.
Potter, Simeon. *Our Language.* Harmondsworth: Penguin Books, 1966.

Works quoted or cited in this book:

Anon. *The Mabinogion,* transl. Gwyn Jones and Thomas Jones. J. M. Dent & Sons, 1949.
Aristotle. *Aristotle on the Art of Poetry,* translated by Ingram Bywater. Oxford, 1920.
Bacon, Francis. *The Advancement of Learning and New Atlantis,* ed. Arthur Johnston. Oxford, 1974.
Bannerman, Helen. *The Story of Little Black Sambo.* Chatto & Windus, 1954.
Borrow, George. *The Works of George Borrow,* ed. Clement Shorter. Constable, 1924.
Boswell, James. *Boswell's Life of Johnson.* Oxford, 1952.
Byron, George Gordon Lord. *Poetical Works.* Oxford, 1945.
Carroll, Lewis. *The Complete Works of Lewis Carroll,* ed. Alexander Woollcott. Nonesuch Press, 1939.
Caxton, William. *Caxton's Eneydos,* ed. Gulley & Furnivall. Oxford, 1980.
Chaucer, Geoffrey. *The Riverside Chaucer,* ed. Larry D. Benson. Oxford, 1988.
Churchill, Winston. *My Early Life.* Fontana Books, 1959.
Corneille, Pierre. *Théâtre Choisi.* Paris: Nelson, 1948.
Croft P. J. *Autograph Poetry in the English Language.* Cassell, 1973.
Dickens, Charles. *Hard Times.* Thomas Nelson & Son Ltd., n.d.

Dickinson, Emily. *Complete Poems*. Boston: Little, Brown & Co., 1960.

Edmond, Lauris. *Selected Poems*. Auckland: Oxford, 1984.

Eliot, Thomas Stearns. *Four Quartets*. New York: Harcourt, Brace & World Inc., 1943.

Fenollosa, Ernest. *The Chinese Written Character as a Medium for Poetry*. ed. Pound. San Francisco: City Lights Books, n.d.

Frame, Janet. *The Envoy from Mirror City*. Auckland: Hutchinson of New Zealand, 1985.

Frost Robert. 'Education by Poetry: A Meditative Monologue' in *The Norton Reader*. New York: W. W. Norton & Co., 1965.

Frye, Northrop. *3 Lectures: University of Toronto Installation Lectures, 1958*. Toronto: University of Toronto Press, 1959.

Gaur, Albertine. *A History of Writing*. The British Library, 1984.

Ghiselin, Brewster. *The Creative Process: a Symposium*. Berkeley: University of California Press, 1952.

Gibbon, Edward. *Memoirs of my Life and Writings,* ed. M. M. Reese. Routledge & Kegan Paul, 1970-71.

Graves, Robert. *Poems of Robert Graves*. New York: Doubleday, 1958.

Hazlitt, William. *The Complete Works of William Hazlitt,* ed. P. P. Howe. J. M. Dent & Sons, 1931.

Herrick, Robert. *Selected Poems*. Grey Walls Press, 1948.

Hopkins, Gerard Manley. *Poems of Gerard Manley Hopkins,* 3rd edition. Oxford, 1948.

Hughes, Ted. *The Hawk in the Rain*. Faber & Faber, 1957.

James, Henry. *The Ambassadors*. J. M. Dent & Sons, 1948.

Johnson, Samuel. *Samuel Johnson*. The Oxford Authors, ed. Greene. Oxford, 1984.

Kipling, Rudyard. *The Collected Works of Rudyard Kipling*. New York: AMS Press, 1970.

Koestler, Arthur. *Arrow in the Blue*. Hutchinson, 1952.

Lane, Margaret. *The Tale of Beatrix Potter*. Fontana Books, 1970.

Locke, John. *An Essay Concerning Human Understanding,* ed. Nidditch. Oxford, 1975.

Mansfield, Katherine. *Journal,* ed. J. Middleton Murry. Constable & Co., 1927.

Milne, A. A. *Winnie-the-Pooh*. Methuen, 1926.

Milton, John. *Complete Works of John Milton*. Oxford, 1959.

Myers, L. M. *The Roots of Modern English*. Boston: Little, Brown & Co., 1966.

O'Connor, Gerard. 'RAFT', *The Manawatu Writing Project*. Palmerston North: Massey University, 1986.

Ogden C. K. and Richards I. A. *The Meaning of Meaning.* Routledge & Kegan Paul, 1923.

Orwell, George. *England Your England and Other Essays.* Secker & Warburg, 1954.

— *Shooting an Elephant and Other Essays.* Secker & Warburg, 1950.

Pope, Alexander. *Poetical Works.* Oxford, 1966.

Pound, Ezra. *ABC of Reading.* Faber & Faber, 1951.

Ratushinskaya, Irina. *Grey is the Colour of Hope.* Hodder & Stoughton, 1988.

Shakespeare, William. *Shakespeare's Sonnets,* ed. Seymour-Smith. Heinemann, 1963.

Sidney, Sir Philip. *Prose Works of Sir Philip Sidney,* ed. Feuillerat. Cambridge, 1962.

Swift, Jonathan. *Gulliver's Travels,* ed. Paul Turner. Oxford, 1971.

Synge, John Millington. *Plays by John M. Synge.* George Allen & Unwin Ltd., 1924.

Twain, Mark. *The Adventures of Huckleberry Finn.* Harmondsworth: Penguin Books, 1966.

Ward, Mary Augusta (Mrs Humphry Ward). *A Writer's Recollections.* W. Collins & Co. Ltd., 1918.

Wilde, Oscar. *The Artist as Critic: Critical Writings of Oscar Wilde,* ed. Ellman. W. H. Allen, 1970.

Wodehouse, Pelham Grenville. *Performing Flea: a Self-Portrait in Letters,* ed. Townend. Harmondsworth: Penguin Books, 1961.

Woolf, Virginia. *A Writer's Diary,* ed. Leonard Woolf. Hogarth Press, 1958.

INDEX